LA TABLE

LA RÂPE

LES CAROTTES

LE TABLIER

LE CONCOMBRE

LE CHOCOLAT

LES VERRES

LES OEUFS

LE THYM

LA POMME

LES BADIANES

LE THERMOS

LE SOLEIL

LES PISTACHES

LES CRAYONS

LA CREVETTE

LES CORNICHONS

LES ASPERGES

LA CASSEROLE

LE COUTEAU

L'OIGNON

LES TOMATES CERISES

LE CHOU

UNE COUPE DE CHAMPAGNE

LES RAISINS

LA LIMONADE

LE BEURRE

LE BLANC D'ŒUF
LE JAUNE D'ŒUF

LE CAFÉ

LA FRAISE

UNE CUILLÈRE À BOIS

LA PLUIE

LA MARYSE

L'HEURE DU DÉJEUNER

LE SEL

LA COQUILLE
SAINT-JACQUES

LE RÉCHAUD À GAZ

LES CERISES

LA COUVERTURE

L'AIL

L'HERBE

LA CRÈME
CHANTILLY

UNE BOUTEILLE
DE VIN

LE FOUET

LA POÊLE

LA GOUSSE
DE VANILLE

UN VERRE
DE VIN

LES OLIVES

The little Paris kitchen

by

Rachel Khoo

The Little Paris Kitchen

Classic French recipes
with a fresh and simple approach

Rachel Khoo

With photography by David Loftus
and illustrations by Rachel Khoo

MICHAEL JOSEPH
an imprint of
Penguin Books

MICHAEL JOSEPH

Published by the Penguin Group

Penguin Books Ltd, 80 Strand, London WC2R 0RL, England

Penguin Group (USA) Inc., 375 Hudson Street, New York,
New York 10014, USA

Penguin Group (Canada), 90 Eglinton Avenue East, Suite 700, Toronto, Ontario, Canada M4P 2Y3
(a division of Pearson Penguin Canada Inc.)

Penguin Ireland, 25 St Stephen's Green, Dublin 2, Ireland
(a division of Penguin Books Ltd)

Penguin Group (Australia), 250 Camberwell Road,
Camberwell, Victoria 3124, Australia (a division of Pearson Australia Group Pty Ltd)

Penguin Books India Pvt Ltd, 11 Community Centre, Panchsheel Park, New Delhi – 110 017, India

Penguin Group (NZ), 67 Apollo Drive, Rosedale, Auckland 0632, New Zealand
(a division of Pearson New Zealand Ltd)

Penguin Books (South Africa) (Pty) Ltd, 24 Sturdee Avenue, Rosebank, Johannesburg 2196, South Africa

Penguin Books Ltd, Registered Offices: 80 Strand, London WC2R 0RL England

www.penguin.com

First published 2012
004

Set in Gill sans and Coquette

Printed in Germany by Mohn media

Colour reproduction by Altaimage Ltd

A CIP catalogue record for this book is available from the British Library

978–0–718–15811–8

www.greenpenguin.co.uk

Penguin Books is committed to a sustainable
future for our business, our readers and our planet.
This book is made from Forest Stewardship
Council™ certified paper.

ALWAYS LEARNING   **PEARSON**

Menu

Introduction

Five years ago, I made the decision to pursue my sweet dream of studying *pâtisserie* at Le Cordon Bleu. So I packed my belongings and waved goodbye to London. A short train journey across the Channel and it was *'Bonjour, Paris'*.

And so my edible Parisian adventure began. The bakeries would entice me with their perfume of freshly baked baguettes and croissants. The cheese-monger would lure me with his perfectly ripe, oozing Brie displayed in the window, conveniently located next to a little wine shop. Its owner, who I nicknamed 'the wine fascist', would interrogate me with a thousand questions in order to find the perfect wine match for my dinners.

The outdoor produce markets overflowed with the season's bounty, brightly coloured fruits and vegetables, and the market traders would shout *'Mademoiselle, goûtez le melon. C'est délicieux!'* ('Miss, taste the melon. It's delicious!') It was a world away from the markets in London and the traders' cockney cries of 'Pound of bananas, a pound!' I soaked up the French ambience in the little cafés and bistros, with the locals sipping their glasses of wine, and watched the world go by.

But discovering *'la vie parisienne'* wasn't just about eating it up. I had some hard work to do. During my first summer in Paris I donned my chef's whites and enrolled at Le Cordon Bleu, the famous cookery school, for a *pâtisserie* course. I said goodbye to my style for the summer, chef's whites not being the most flattering of women's attire. Not even Kate Moss could make them look good! It was *'Oui, chef'* for the next three months, while I learned how to make French classics like croissants and *crème brûlée*. Two hundred eggs and 20 kilos of butter, sugar and flour later, I graduated from Le Cordon Bleu. Not quite ready to give up my sweet dream of living in Paris, I started to work at a small culinary bookstore, La Cocotte, where I baked delicious delicacies for the *salon du thé* and catered for their book launches. My little baking job led me to my current vocation as a food creative, where I develop culinary ideas for events, cookbooks, workshops and anything else food-related. All the testing is done from the tiny little kitchen in my apartment with just a mini oven and two gas rings.

Somehow the rest of the world has forgotten how *'délicieux'* French food can be. The food headlines have been dominated by El Bulli's molecular movement in Spain, Heston Blumenthal's edible English eccentricities or, more recently, Scandinavia's flourishing foraging scene showcased at Noma. French cuisine has been forgone, stereotyped with the stuffy image of an old-fashioned chef labouring over a terribly complicated dish, finished with a ton of butter.

'Mais non!' I say. French flavours and techniques needn't be out of reach of the everyday home cook. Living in Paris, I eat and cook everything from simple everyday suppers to big gourmet dinners. And just because they use fancy words like *'jus'* or *'blanchir'* doesn't mean you have to have a Michelin-starred kitchen to cook great French food. I certainly don't and have managed to cook up everything from feasts for six, to girlie tea parties for eight and romantic three-course dinners for two.

My book includes all the well-known French dishes such as *Boeuf bourguignon* and *Coq au vin,* but it's not simply another collection of classics. It's the story of how I discovered these recipes, whether it was picnicking along the Seine on a sticky summer's night, dining with friends or experimenting at home. I have added my own creative twist on some occasions, making this book a fresh and simple approach to French classics, perfect to share with friends and family.

Bienvenue dans ma petite cuisine à Paris!

Rachel

LES ASPERGES   LA VAISSELLE   LES PIMENTS   LA CREVETTE   LES BADIANES   LE CHOU

LA COQUILLE SAINT-JACQUES   LE THYM   LES POMMES DE TERRE   LE POULET   LES POIVRONS   LE FENOUIL

LA LAVANDE

LA CARAFE D'EAU

Everyday Cooking

Ma cuisine de tous les jours

LE FENOUIL

LES BOUGIES

LA CREVETTE

LES FEUILLES DE LAURIER

LA CARAFE D'EAU   L'OIGNON   LES BADIANES   LE THYM   LA VAISSELLE   LES CAROTTES

LES BOUGIES   LA COQUILLE SAINT-JACQUES   LE CHOU   LES PIMENTS   LES POMMES DE TERRE   LES ASPERGES

There is much to be said about the daily eating habits of the French. Simplicity and *savoir faire* and an understanding of ingredients are key. Generally, a steaming cup of *café au lait* with a sweet and comforting croissant are grabbed *en route* to work for breakfast. Dinners for family and friends are important events, so dishes for these occasions have a chapter of their own (see page 152), which leaves us with lunch. I wanted to call this chapter 'Everyday Cooking' as it features simple things that are mostly eaten for lunch or supper.

'*L'heure de déjeuner*' – the French lunch hour – according to the stereotype consists of several courses, a couple of bottles of wine and takes half an afternoon. Unfortunately the days of leisurely lunches during the week are a thing of the past as even the French aren't immune to the working culture. '*Le sandwich*' is, therefore, fast becoming the norm for a weekday lunch, although the French do know how to make an excellent '*jambon–beurre*', also called a '*parisienne*' – a crusty baguette slathered in rich creamy butter with a slice of juicy ham. Not much to it, but it does beat a soggy sandwich any day.

When life does allow a longer lunch break, a visit to the local bistro or neighbourhood café is the norm. The local eateries know what their customers want to eat: food to comfort the nerves after a stressful morning at the office. *Moules marinières*, *steak tartare*, *gratin dauphinois*, *saucisse et purée de pomme de terre avec une sauce diable* (bangers 'n' mash with devil's sauce), *oeufs en cocotte* (baked eggs). No fancy fussed-about food here.

While I was writing this book, I decided to test some of the recipes out on the public by opening up my own 'underground' restaurant for just two diners, as my apartment is so small. People from all over the world (including the French) booked in and came for lunch. It soon became clear that, no matter what nationality they were, the thing they loved most was the fact that it was simple home-cooked food, not Michelin-starred gastronomy. Food that any Pierre, Paul or Jacques (Tom, Dick or Harry!) can cook at home.

So roll up your sleeves and get stuck in to a little kitchen work or, as they say in French, '*mettre la main à la pâte*' ('put your hand in the dough') and you'll be rewarded with an everyday meal worth sitting down to.

Salade de figues et foies de volailles

Fig and chicken liver salad

When figs appear at my local market (the best figs are available from July to September in France), I just have to buy them. Sweet, sticky and juicy, they often don't even make it back to my kitchen — I usually gobble them all up on my way home — but if there are a few remaining, they make a delicious addition to a salad.

The sweetness of figs goes particularly well with cheese and also chicken livers. I was never a big liver fan as a kid, but they have grown on me since living in France, especially as they take literally no time to cook. Fast food *à la française*!

• 1 tablespoon butter • 1 red onion, thinly sliced • 1 sprig of thyme
• 200g chicken livers, cleaned (if the livers are quite large, cut them in half)
• salt and pepper • 2 tablespoons red wine vinegar • 100g mixed salad leaves
• 4 figs, quartered • extra virgin olive oil, for drizzling

Melt the butter in a large non-stick frying pan and add the onion and thyme. Fry on a medium heat for about 6–8 minutes or until the onion becomes soft and slightly caramelized.

Season the livers with salt and pepper. Turn the heat up to high before adding the livers to the pan, then fry for about 1–2 minutes on each side or until golden brown on the outside but still pink in the middle. Add the wine vinegar at the end and let it evaporate for 30 seconds.

While the livers are cooking, scatter the salad leaves and figs on a plate.

Top the salad with the onion and livers (discarding the thyme), followed by a drizzle of olive oil and a sprinkle of salt.

Preparation time: 10 minutes   Cooking time: 15 minutes

Lentilles du Puy avec un fromage de chèure, betteraves et une vinaigrette d'aneth

Puy lentil salad with goat's cheese, beetroot and a dill vinaigrette

Lentilles du Puy are grown in the sunny, volcanic Auvergne. The hot climate and mineral-rich soil give them a unique taste and texture, and they are known in France as poor man's caviar. They contain less starch than ordinary green lentils, so they hold their shape better: no mushy *lentilles du Puy*. Traditionally they are boiled in water, then fried with some chopped onion and *lardons*. I tend to improvize with ingredients I have in the fridge: they make a fine accompaniment to almost anything.

• 200g Puy lentils • 1 bay leaf • 1 sprig of thyme • salt and pepper • 1 cooked beetroot, peeled
• a handful of baby salad leaves (optional) • 200g fresh soft goat's cheese* • extra virgin olive oil

For the dill vinaigrette • ½ bunch of dill • 2 tablespoons sunflower oil
• 2 tablespoons white wine vinegar • ½ teaspoon salt • a pinch of sugar

Wash the lentils in cold running water, then put them into a large pot with the bay leaf, thyme and a generous pinch of salt. Cover the lentils with at least double their volume of boiling water and cook for 15 minutes or until tender.

Meanwhile, make the *vinaigrette* by whizzing the dill (stalks included) in an electric blender with all the other ingredients. Taste and add more salt if desired.

Use a mandoline or a sharp knife to thinly slice the beetroot.

Drain the lentils and discard the bay leaf and thyme.

To assemble, divide the lentils equally between individual plates (or you could use a large serving dish) and scatter over the salad leaves (if using). Place the beetroot slices on top and crumble over the goat's cheese. Drizzle with the *vinaigrette* and a little olive oil, and finish with a sprinkling of salt and pepper.

* *If you prefer a stronger-tasting cheese, try feta or a hard goat's cheese.*

Preparation time: 20 minutes   Cooking time: 15–20 minutes

Salade tiède de pommes de terre et pommes avec des miettes de boudin noir

Warm potato and apple salad with black-pudding crumbs

Before I moved to France, the thought of eating *boudin noir* (blood sausage or black pudding) would have made my stomach turn, but now I must admit I'm quite partial to a slice or two.

If you're a *boudin noir* virgin and feel a little intimidated about eating a whole sausage, then this dish is a great way to try it because there's only a small amount and it's used like a garnish.

In France, *boudin noir* is usually partnered with cooked apples and potatoes, making it the perfect cold-weather comfort food. This recipe has the addition of mint, to give it a fresh flavour.

• 1 teaspoon olive oil • 250g waxy potatoes (e.g Maris Peer or Charlotte), chopped into small cubes • salt and pepper • 1 Granny Smith apple • 1 tablespoon water • 1 teaspoon sugar • a handful of mint leaves • 125g *boudin noir* or black pudding

Put the olive oil into a pan and place on a medium heat. When the pan is warm, add the cubed potatoes and cook for 10 minutes or until the potatoes are tender and a lovely golden-brown colour. Shake the pan every now and again, and season the potatoes with salt and pepper.

Meanwhile, peel three-quarters of the apple and chop into small cubes (save the remainder for later). Microwave the apple cubes with the water and sugar in a covered bowl until soft. This should only take a minute or two. (Alternatively, cook for about 5 minutes in a covered small pot.)

Using the back of a tablespoon, mash the cooked apple to a purée, then keep the purée covered so that it stays warm.

Finely chop the mint and chop the remaining apple into small cubes (leave the skin on).

Once the potatoes are cooked, pop them into a bowl and keep them covered. Place the pan back on a medium heat. Remove the skin from the sausage and crumble the sausagemeat into the pan. Cook for 2–3 minutes, tossing the crumbs so that they brown evenly.

To plate up, start by spreading a tablespoon of the apple purée on each plate. Sprinkle over a little of the mint, followed by the potatoes, sausage crumbs and chopped apple. Finally, sprinkle with a little more mint. Serve immediately.

Preparation time: 30 minutes Cooking time: 20 minutes

Salade d'hiver avec une mousse au fromage de chèvre

Winter salad with a goat's cheese mousse

The Paris des Chefs conference is a draw for international culinary talent and is always inspirational. At the 2011 conference I met Estonian chef Peeter Pihel (from Neh in Tallinn and Pädaste Manor on Muhu Island) and tasted one of his dishes – roasted root vegetables with a goat's cheese mousse. It inspired me to try something similar with produce from my local Parisian market.

This recipe can be adapted to any vegetables that are in season, and in summer you can use peppers, cucumbers and tomatoes to make a crunchy raw version.

• 4 carrots, roughly chopped • 2 small dessert apples, cored and quartered
• 2 parsnips, roughly chopped • 2 tablespoons sunflower oil • salt
• 100g *lardons* or of smoked bacon (optional)
• 1 cooked beetroot, peeled and very thinly sliced • 2 handfuls of salad leaves

For the mousse • 200g *Selles-sur-Cher* cheese* • 8 tablespoons milk • 250ml whipping cream

For the vinaigrette • 4 tablespoons sunflower or vegetable oil • 2 tablespoons cider vinegar • salt

Preheat the oven to 200°C. Toss the carrots, apples and parsnips into a large roasting tin. Drizzle with the sunflower oil and season with salt. Roast for 45 minutes or until the vegetables are tender and golden.

Meanwhile, make the mousse. Beat the cheese with the milk until soft and lump-free. Whip the cream to stiff peaks. Add one-quarter of the whipped cream to the cheese and mix together, then fold in the rest of the cream. Transfer the mousse to a piping bag fitted with a 1cm plain nozzle and leave in the fridge until needed (it will keep for a couple of days).

Make the *vinaigrette* by mixing together the oil and vinegar with salt to taste.

Just as the vegetables finish cooking, toss the *lardons* (if using) into a hot pan and cook until crisp.

To serve, pipe little blobs of mousse randomly all over a serving plate. Arrange the roasted vegetables and apples, beetroot and salad leaves on the plate, and sprinkle the *lardons* (if used) on top. Finally, drizzle with the *vinaigrette*.

* Selles-sur-Cher cheese *works particularly well. It is a goat's cheese coated in edible ash that lends a subtle smokiness. But any other soft goat's cheese will also work.*

Preparation time: 30 minutes   Cooking time: 45 minutes

Poireaux vinaigrette avec oeuf poché et jambon de Bayonne

Leeks in vinaigrette with a poached egg and Bayonne ham

The Italians have Parma ham and the Spanish have Serrano, while the French have *jambon de Bayonne*, named after the city in south-west France. It is air-dried for months, while it goes through various salt-, fat- and spice-rubbing processes to make a delicate meat that is slightly sweet and moist. Bayonne ham makes a great addition to the classic *poireaux vinaigrette*, which you don't see much any more, unless you happen to have a French *grand-mère*. Normally the leeks are boiled or steamed, but I like to pop them on the griddle pan. It brings out their sweetness.

• 8 young leeks • 3 tablespoons olive oil • 1 egg per person • 4 slices of Bayonne ham*
• a couple of drops of vinegar

For the vinaigrette • 6 tablespoons sunflower oil • 3 tablespoons white wine vinegar
• 2 teaspoons grainy mustard • a pinch of sugar • salt

Trim the roots and remove the tough tops and outer leaves from the leeks. Cut the leeks in half lengthways and soak in cold water for 10 minutes, then rinse to remove any grit that may be in between the leaves.

Heat a griddle pan until smoking hot.

Brush the cut side of each leek half with olive oil, then place the leeks cut-side down in the pan and cook for 5 minutes or until the grill marks appear. Brush the top side of the leeks before turning them over to cook for a further 5 minutes.

Meanwhile, bring a large pot of water to a boil. Crack an egg into a ramekin or cup and add a drop of vinegar. Whisk the boiling water vigorously before slipping in the egg, then quickly repeat with more eggs and poach for 3–4 minutes until the yolks are just set and slightly soft.

Mix together the ingredients for the *vinaigrette*, adding salt to taste.

To assemble, divide the leeks between individual plates and drizzle the *vinaigrette* on top.** Shred the ham into strips and drape over the leeks. Top each serving with a poached egg and a sprinkling of salt.

* Can be substituted with Serrano or Parma ham.

** The leeks and vinaigrette can be served on their own as a hot side dish, or cold the next day.

Preparation time: 30 minutes Cooking time: 20 minutes

Oeufs en meurette

Poached eggs in a red wine sauce

This is a pretty classy way to serve a humble poached egg for an indulgent brunch or starter for lunch. Both the sauce and the eggs can be prepared a day in advance.

• 4 fresh eggs*

*For the red wine sauce*** • 1 onion, finely chopped • 1 stick of celery, finely chopped
• 1 carrot, finely chopped • 30g *lardons* or cubes of smoked bacon • 30g butter
• 30g plain flour • 500ml veal or beef stock, warm • 1 tablespoon tomato paste
• 175ml red wine • 1 bouquet garni (thyme, bay leaf, parsley stalks, peppercorns)

To make the sauce, fry the vegetables and *lardons* on a medium heat until golden. Remove them from the pan with a slotted spoon, then add the butter. Melt over a medium heat, sprinkle in the flour and stir constantly until it turns an almost Coca-Cola colour. Turn the heat down to low and slowly pour in the warm stock, whisking energetically. Add the tomato paste and wine and whisk until the paste has dissolved. Pop the fried vegetables and *lardons* back into the pan, add the bouquet garni and simmer gently for 15 minutes. Pour the sauce through a sieve and taste for seasoning, then pour into a clean pan and gently heat through.

Meanwhile, pour water into a deep, wide frying pan until about 8cm deep and bring to a boil. Crack each egg into a ramekin or cup and add a drop of vinegar. Whisk the boiling water vigorously before quickly slipping in the eggs one after the other. Turn the heat down and simmer for 3–4 minutes or until the yolks are just set and slightly soft.

Remove the eggs from the water with a slotted spoon and serve on hot toast, with the sauce poured over and around.***

* *The key to successful poaching is to use the freshest eggs possible. Old eggs will have ragged, feathery whites, whereas the white on a fresh egg will hold together.*

** *For a fiery sauce, add 10 cracked black peppercorns.*

*** *To make in advance, put the poached eggs into a bowl of ice-cold water and pour the sauce into an airtight container. Keep both in the fridge. Reheat the sauce before serving, and warm the eggs through by lowering them into boiling water with a slotted spoon. Simmer for 30 seconds.*

Preparation time: 15 minutes   Cooking time: 30 minutes

Oeufs en cocotte

Eggs in pots

Two main ingredients – eggs and *crème fraîche* – are all you need for this super-simple yet very tasty dish. You can glam it up with a drizzle of truffle oil at the end if you like, or with a few thin shavings of real truffle.

I usually take a look in my fridge and throw in whatever I find suitable (which is almost anything savoury). Serve with plenty of crusty bread or, for a gluten-free alternative, try steamed asparagus, raw carrot, pepper or cucumber sticks.

Traditionally ramekins are used for baking *oeufs en cocotte*, but I make mine in teacups to add a little British touch to this classic French dish.

• 150g *crème fraîche** • salt and pepper • nutmeg • a handful of chopped dill** • 4 eggs

For the optional garnish • red lumpfish roe • small sprigs of dill

Preheat the oven to 180°C. Season the *crème fraîche* with salt, pepper and a pinch of nutmeg. Place a heaped tablespoon of *crème fraîche* in the bottom of a ramekin, followed by a little dill. Crack an egg on top, add a second tablespoon of *crème fraîche* and sprinkle with a pinch each of salt, pepper and nutmeg. Repeat with 3 more ramekins.

Place the ramekins in a baking dish and pour enough lukewarm water into the dish to come halfway up the sides of the ramekins. Bake for 15 minutes or until the egg yolks are set to your liking.

If you like, finish each serving with a teaspoon of red lumpfish roe and a sprig or two of dill.

Some alternative ideas:

* *The* crème fraîche *can be replaced with* Sauce Béchamel *or* Sauce Mornay *(see page 269). If you like, you can add chopped mushrooms, ham, smoked salmon or cherry tomatoes after the* crème fraîche, *or a spoonful of* piperade *(see page 30).*

** Try swapping the dill for parsley, basil or coriander, or spice things up with a dash of Tabasco or chilli sauce.

Preparation time: 10 minutes Baking time: 15 minutes

Omelette soufflée et piperade

Soufflé omelette with a Basque pepper relish

The Basque region in the western Pyrenées has a strong identity, which is reflected in its food. In *piperade*, the colours of tomatoes, green pepper and onion represent the red, green and white of the Basque flag.

Traditionally *piperade* is made with eggs that are simply scrambled into the dish, but I like to go the extra mile and serve it as a fluffy soufflé omelette.

For the piperade • 2 tablespoons olive oil • 1 clove of garlic, crushed to a paste
• 1 onion, thinly sliced • 1 sprig of thyme • 1 green pepper, deseeded and thinly sliced
• ½ teaspoon ground Espelette pepper* or a pinch of regular chilli powder
• 2 tomatoes, roughly chopped • a pinch of sugar • salt

For the soufflé omelette • 4 eggs, separated • a pinch of salt • 1 tablespoon butter

To make the *piperade,*** place a large non-stick pan on a medium heat and put the olive oil, garlic, onion and thyme into the pan. When the onion begins to soften, throw in the green pepper, Espelette pepper and tomatoes. Cover and cook for 10 minutes or until the green pepper is soft.

Meanwhile, preheat the oven to 180°C and make the soufflé omelette. Put the egg whites and salt into a bowl and beat until stiff. In a separate large bowl, beat the egg yolks for a minute. Fold half the egg whites into the egg yolks until evenly incorporated, then fold in the rest.

Place a large non-stick frying pan (that can go in the oven) on a medium heat. Melt the butter until it begins to sizzle, then pour in the eggs and spread them quickly with a palette knife to cover the bottom of the pan. Cook for 3–4 minutes, then place in the oven and bake for 4 minutes.

To serve, loosen the omelette from the bottom of the pan with the palette knife. Invert a large plate on top of the pan, then turn the pan and plate over so the omelette comes out on the plate. Remove the sprig of thyme from the *piperade*, add the sugar and taste for seasoning. Spread the *piperade* on top of the omelette and serve immediately.

Espelette pepper is cultivated in the Basque country, which is why it's so commonly used in the cuisine of this region. Don't be misled by its bright orange-red colour – it is slightly less fiery then chilli (but it does have a bit more kick than regular pepper).

** *The* piperade *can be made up to 3 days in advance and kept in the fridge, then reheated before spreading on top of the omelette. It is also good served cold with crusty bread or a dollop of crème fraîche.*

Preparation time: 10 minutes   Cooking time: 20 minutes

Soupe au pistou

Pistou soup

Soup is not just for cold winter nights, it's great for hot summer days too. *Soupe au pistou*, from Provence, is jam-packed with summer vegetables and is served with a sauce – the *pistou* part. *Pistou* is a distant relative of the Italian *pesto*, except that *pistou* traditionally has no pine nuts or Parmesan cheese (the word originates from the Provençal dialect and means pounded). If you don't have a mortar and pestle for the pounding, some simple whizzing in a blender will give you a pretty good result too. Maybe the modern version should be called *soupe au whizzou*?

• 3 tablespoons olive oil • 2 onions, diced • 4 cloves of garlic, crushed to a paste • 1 sprig of thyme • 2 bay leaves • 4 tablespoons tomato paste • 2 carrots, diced • 2 courgettes, diced • 200g green beans, quartered • 400g tin white beans (e.g. haricots blancs, cannellini), drained and rinsed • 2 litres boiling water • 1 tablespoon salt • a pinch of sugar • pepper • 100g dried pasta (a small variety like orzo) • 200g fresh or frozen peas

For a classic pistou • 1 bunch of basil • 3 cloves of garlic • 3–4 tablespoons good extra virgin olive oil

For a Vietnamese pistou • 1 bunch of Vietnamese basil • 1 stalk of lemongrass, roughly chopped • ½ small red chilli, deseeded • 5 tablespoons sunflower oil

To make the *pistou*, simply pound the ingredients to a smooth paste (or whizz in an electric blender).

To make the soup, heat the olive oil in a large pot. Add the onions and garlic and cook gently, stirring occasionally, until soft and translucent. Add the thyme, bay leaves, tomato paste, carrots and courgettes, then cook for 15–20 minutes or until the vegetables are *al dente* (tender but still a little crunchy). Add the green and white beans with the boiling water and bring to a boil, then add the pasta and peas. Cook for 10 minutes or until the pasta is *al dente*. Remove the sprig of thyme and the bay leaves, then add the salt and sugar plus pepper to taste. Serve immediately, with a dollop of the pistou.

Pourquoi a Vietnamese pistou?

This spicy *pistou* is a homage to Le Grain du Riz, one of my favourite Vietnamese restaurants in Paris (if you can call it a restaurant – it only seats 12 people). When Vietnam was a French colony, the Vietnamese adopted the *baguette*, and a popular snack is *bánh mì*, a *baguette* filled with mayonnaise, various pickled vegetables and grilled meat. Now it seems the tables have turned, and the Vietnamese community in France is influencing the French culinary scene with cheap and cheerful *cantines* popping up everywhere.

Preparation time: 30 minutes Cooking time: 35–40 minutes

Gratin dauphinois

Creamy potato bake

To rinse or not to rinse the potatoes, that is the question that pops up in many *gratin dauphinois* recipes. It all depends whether you're using waxy or floury potatoes. Floury ones will release their starch into the cream and make the gratin bind, whereas I prefer waxy potatoes as they hold their shape better (no gratin mush for me). I like my gratin to be dense with crunchy, crisp edges, but you could always conduct some potato experiments of your own. All for research purposes, of course, not the fact that it's so delicious . . .

• 1kg waxy potatoes, e.g. Maris Peer or Charlotte • 300ml milk • 300ml double cream
• a pinch of nutmeg • 1 teaspoon Dijon mustard • 1 teaspoon salt • 1 clove of garlic
• a knob of soft butter • chopped parsley or dill (optional)

Peel the potatoes and cut them into 3mm-thick slices. Place them in a pot with the milk, cream, nutmeg, mustard and salt, and simmer for 10 minutes.

Meanwhile, preheat the oven to 200°C. Cut the clove of garlic in half and rub the cut sides around the inside of a baking dish, then smear the knob of butter around the inside of the dish.

Pour the potato and cream mix into the dish and spread the potatoes out evenly. Bake for 35–40 minutes or until golden and bubbling. Serve hot, topped with a sprinkling of chopped parsley or dill if you like, and a simple green salad.

For a light lunch or dinner for 4–6 people
Stir 200g chopped smoked salmon, the finely grated zest of an unwaxed lemon and a handful of chopped dill into the potato mix before baking.

Preparation time: 15 minutes Cooking time: 45–50 minutes

Nids de tartiflette

Cheese and potato nests

The *tartiflette* recipe was the brainchild of the Reblochon cheese producers in the 1980s. With so many other French cheeses to compete with, they needed to find a way of making theirs more popular, and they did it with this cheesy potato gratin.

Reblochon is a cheese that comes from the Haute-Savoie in the Alps. It's made out of raw cow's milk, has a pungent aroma and nutty taste. If you can't find Reblochon, or you prefer a milder flavour, replace it with Brie and make a *Brieflette* (doesn't have quite the same ring, though, does it?).

Traditionally this dish is quite a heavy winter staple, but make it my way and you can even serve it on a hot day with a side salad.

• 1 tablespoon soft butter • 500g waxy potatoes, e.g. Maris Peer or Charlotte
• 1 onion, finely chopped • 1 clove of garlic, finely chopped • 1 bay leaf
• 200g *lardons* or cubes of smoked bacon • 100ml dry white wine
• 250g piece of Reblochon cheese, cubed

Preheat the oven to 180°C and brush a 6-hole muffin tin with the soft butter. Peel the potatoes and use the *julienne* blade on a mandoline to make thin matchsticks (or slice by hand).

Put the onion, garlic, bay leaf and *lardons* into a large non-stick frying pan and cook until the *lardons* are golden. Add the wine and reduce until only a couple of tablespoons of liquid remain. Stir in the potato matchsticks and take off the heat, then remove the bay leaf and stir in the Reblochon cubes.

Divide the potato mix between the 6 holes in the muffin tin and bake for 15–20 minutes or until golden and bubbling.

Preparation time: 30 minutes   Baking time: 15–20 minutes

Gratin de choufleur avec une chapelure aux noisettes

Cauliflower bake with hazelnut crunch crust

Béchamel sauce with the addition of cheese (called *sauce Mornay* by the French) can only be a good thing. Coat any kind of vegetable with this sauce, and it'll get vegetable-hating kids licking their plates clean. A sneaky little trick I learned during my years working as a nanny.

The cauliflower can easily be replaced with broccoli, sliced courgettes, pumpkin or even potatoes.

- 1.5kg head of cauliflower, trimmed and separated into florets (about 1kg when trimmed)
- 50g hazelnuts, finely chopped • 1 slice of extra-crunchy toast, roughly chopped

For the cheese (Mornay) sauce • 30g butter • 30g plain flour • 500ml milk, lukewarm
• ¼ onion, skin removed • 1 clove • 1 bay leaf • a pinch each of white pepper and nutmeg
• salt • 200g Gruyère or mature Comté and Parmesan cheese, grated

Steam the cauliflower using either a steamer basket or a colander fitted inside a pan. Cooking time depends on how you like your cauliflower cooked – I like mine on the crunchy side, which takes about 15 minutes.

Meanwhile, make the sauce. Melt the butter in a large pan over a medium heat. Add the flour and beat hard until you have a smooth paste. Take off the heat and leave to cool for 2 minutes, then gradually add the milk, whisking constantly. Place the pan back over a medium heat, add the onion, clove and bay leaf and simmer gently for 10 minutes, whisking frequently. If the sauce becomes too thick, whisk in a little more milk. Finish the sauce by removing the onion, clove and bay leaf, then add the pepper and nutmeg and salt to taste. Leave to cool slightly.

Preheat the oven to 180°C.

Stir the cheese into the warm sauce (save a little to sprinkle on top of the gratin), then mix the sauce with the cauliflower and spoon into individual baking dishes.* Sprinkle with the rest of the cheese followed by the hazelnuts and toast crumbs. Bake for 10 minutes, then pop under a hot grill for a few minutes to get a golden, bubbling crust.

* Or bake in 1 large dish for 20 minutes, followed by about 5 minutes under the grill.

Preparation time: 30 minutes Cooking time: 30 minutes

Gratin de macaronis au fromage

Mac 'n' cheese

My first job in Paris was taking care of two girls, Kami and Loïs. Cooking for French tastebuds is daunting enough, and cooking for kids can be even harder, but this dish was a winner every time I made it. A great thing considering how easy it is to make, with ingredients that you're most likely to have to hand in the kitchen.

• 300g macaroni • 200g Gruyère, mature Comté or Parmesan cheese,* grated

For the Béchamel *sauce* • 30g butter • 30g plain flour • 500ml milk, lukewarm
• ¼ onion, skin removed • 1 clove • 1 bay leaf • a pinch of nutmeg • salt and white pepper

To make the béchamel sauce, melt the butter in a large pan over a medium heat. Add the flour and beat hard until you have a smooth paste. Take off the heat and leave to cool for 2 minutes, then gradually add the milk, whisking constantly. Place the pan back over a medium heat, add the onion, clove and bay leaf and simmer gently for 10 minutes, whisking frequently. If the sauce becomes too thick, whisk in a little more milk.

While the sauce is simmering, preheat the oven to 180°C and cook the pasta according to packet instructions.

Finish the sauce by removing the onion, clove and bay leaf, then adding the nutmeg and seasoning with salt and white pepper (although black pepper is fine if you don't mind the speckles). Leave to cool slightly.

Drain the pasta and tip into a large baking dish.

Save a handful of cheese to sprinkle on the top at the end, then mix the rest into the warm sauce.** Pour the sauce over the pasta and mix until the pasta is well coated. Sprinkle the rest of the cheese on top and bake for 20 minutes until bubbly and golden.

Pourquoi? *It's important to use a strong-flavoured cheese as you will need less cheese to give the sauce a good flavour.*

** *Make sure you add the cheese when the sauce is warm rather than hot. If the sauce is too hot, the fat will separate from the protein and form a layer on top.*

Preparation time: 15 minutes   Cooking time: 35 minutes

Ratatouille

Provençal vegetable stew

How to make a *ratatouille* can be a touchy subject at dinner parties in France, with everyone claiming their recipe is the best. Some people prefer to cook each vegetable individually and mix everything together at the end, others prefer to throw it all in a pot, and then there are some who like to carefully arrange the vegetables and make a sort of gratin. At the end of the day it all depends whether you like your *ratatouille* soft and jammy or with a bit of bite.

Of course, being someone who wants to have it all, I like my *ratatouille* to tick both boxes. Part-cooking the vegetables on top of the stove and then baking everything together in the oven gives you the best of both worlds – creamy soft onion and tomatoes, with freshness and crunch from the courgette and peppers.

• 1 clove of garlic, crushed to a paste • 1 onion, finely chopped • 1 sprig of thyme, leaves only
• 3 tablespoons olive oil, plus extra for drizzling • 1 aubergine, thinly sliced*
• 1 courgette, thinly sliced* • 1 red pepper, deseeded and thinly sliced • 1 yellow pepper,
deseeded and thinly sliced • 6 tomatoes, cut into quarters • a pinch of sugar • salt

Preheat the oven to 180°C. Gently fry the garlic, onion and thyme leaves in 2 tablespoons of the olive oil. Once the onion is translucent and soft, add the aubergine and continue to cook until soft (roughly 5 minutes).

Toss the remaining vegetables in a large roasting tin with another tablespoon of olive oil. Add the cooked onion and aubergine and mix together.

Cover the roasting tin with aluminium foil (making sure the foil doesn't touch the vegetables) or with baking paper. Bake for an hour, then stir the vegetables a little and add the sugar. Taste for salt. Set under a hot grill for 3–4 minutes or until the top layer of vegetables is caramelized around the edges. Drizzle with olive oil and serve warm, or cold the next day.

A mandoline makes an easy job of cutting vegetables into thin slices.

Preparation time: 30 minutes Cooking time: 1¼ hours

Lapin croustillant à la moutarde de Meaux

Crispy rabbit with Meaux mustard

It was the Romans who introduced mustard seeds to the Gauls, and by the ninth century monasteries all over France were making money from selling mustard. The stone quarries in the Meaux region provided the millstones to grind the mustard seeds, turning the area into one of the top French mustard producers, and yet *moutarde de Meaux* is probably less well known than its southern relative – the spicy yellow mustard from Dijon.

Unlike Dijon mustard, which is creamy, the grains in the traditional mustard from Meaux are only partially ground, giving it a crunch that makes a great crispy crust when combined with breadcrumbs.

- 2 tablespoons vegetable or sunflower oil • 4 rabbit legs*
- 4 heaped tablespoons Meaux mustard or another grainy mustard
- 50g breadcrumbs (fresh or dried)

Preheat the oven to 200°C. Swirl the oil around a roasting tray and place in the oven to get hot.

Meanwhile, brush the rabbit legs with plenty of mustard and then press the breadcrumbs on to the mustard to coat the rabbit evenly.

Place the rabbit legs on the hot baking tray and roast for 30 minutes or until cooked through. The juices should run clear, not red or pink, when a thick part of the flesh is pierced with the tip of a sharp knife. Serve hot.

* Chicken legs are also good cooked this way.

Preparation time: 15 minutes Cooking time: 30 minutes

Moules marinières

Mussels with white wine

There's not much you need to make *moules marinières*. Add a splash of white wine to some softened onion, throw in the mussels and finish with a dollop of *crème fraîche* – that's more or less it. Who said French food was complicated?

• 2kg mussels • 1 onion, thinly sliced • 1 bulb of fennel, thinly sliced* • 1 tablespoon butter
• 1 bay leaf • 2 sprigs of thyme or a pinch of dried thyme • 160ml dry white wine
• 160g *crème fraîche* • a handful of chopped parsley

Clean the mussels using plenty of cold water. Pull out the fibrous beards and scrub off any barnacles. Toss any that have cracked or broken shells, or that do not close when lightly squeezed.

In a large pot (big enough to hold all the mussels with some extra room to spare), soften the onion and fennel over a low heat with the butter, bay leaf and thyme. When the onion and fennel are soft and translucent, add the wine followed by the cleaned mussels. Increase the heat to high, cover the pan and cook for 3–4 minutes or until the mussels open, shaking the pan a few times to help them cook evenly.

At the end of the cooking time, remove the bay leaf and sprigs of thyme (if used) and discard any mussels that have not opened. Stir in the *crème fraîche* and serve immediately, with a sprinkling of chopped parsley – and some crusty bread.

* *I've included the fennel because it adds a subtle aniseed flavour that goes extremely well with the white wine and* crème fraîche, *but you don't have to use it.*

Preparation time: 15 minutes Cooking time: 10 minutes

Gratin au poisson fumé

Smoky fish bake

This easy bake makes good use of leftover cooked potatoes. You can also mix in leftover vegetables such as courgettes, carrots, broccoli and cauliflower.

• 750g (8–10 medium) potatoes, peeled and already cooked (you can use leftover roast potatoes)
• 200g smoked haddock, skin removed • a handful of chopped parsley
• a handful of grated mature cheese, e.g. Gruyere, Comté, Parmesan or mature Cheddar

For the Béchamel sauce • 30g butter • 30g plain flour • 500ml milk, lukewarm
• ¼ onion, skin removed • 1 clove • 1 bay leaf • a pinch of nutmeg • salt and white pepper

To make the béchamel sauce, melt the butter in a large pan over a medium heat. Add the flour and beat hard until you have a smooth paste. Take off the heat and leave to cool for 2 minutes, then gradually add the milk, whisking constantly. Place the pan back over a medium heat, add the onion, clove and bay leaf and simmer gently for 10 minutes, whisking frequently. If the sauce becomes too thick, whisk in a little more milk. Finish the sauce by removing the onion, clove and bay leaf, then adding the nutmeg and seasoning with salt and white pepper (although black pepper is fine if you don't mind the speckles). Leave to cool slightly.

Preheat the oven to 180°C.

Slice the potatoes into ½cm-thick rounds. Cut or flake the haddock into small chunks and add to the béchamel sauce with most of the parsley (save a little for garnish). Mix together, then add the potatoes. Pour into a baking dish, sprinkle with a little grated cheese and bake for 20 minutes or until golden. Garnish with a little chopped parsley before serving.

Preparation time: 15 minutes Cooking time: 35 minutes

Truite en papillote avec fenouil, citron et crème fraîche

Trout in a parcel with lemon, fennel and *crème fraîche*

Papillote sounds a lot more fancy than it actually is – ingredients simply popped into a paper parcel and then baked. The only thing to remember is to seal your parcel well, so that none of the delicious juices can escape.

• 300g baby potatoes, scrubbed • 4 tablespoons extra virgin olive oil
• finely grated zest of 1 unwaxed lemon • salt and pepper
• 2 freshwater trout, cleaned and gutted (with bones left in) • 1 bulb of fennel, thinly sliced

For serving • 4 heaped tablespoons *crème fraîche* • lemon wedges

Steam the potatoes until almost tender, roughly 10 minutes. Leave until cool enough to handle, then slice. Preheat the oven to 170°C.

Mix the olive oil with the lemon zest and 1 teaspoon salt and pepper to taste. Rub this mixture inside the fish.

Place each trout on a large sheet of baking paper and stuff with the fennel slices. Place the sliced potatoes on the paper, alongside the fish. Now bring the edges of the paper together and fold over to form a sealed parcel, tucking the ends underneath. You may need to use kitchen string or aluminium foil to keep each parcel closed.

Bake for 15–20 minutes, depending on the thickness of the fish. To test for doneness, open a parcel and lift up the skin of the fish – the flesh should look opaque, not translucent, and flake easily with a fork. Serve with the juices from the parcels, the *crème fraîche* and lemon wedges.

Preparation time: 15 minutes Cooking time: 25–30 minutes

Tartare de maquereau avec un condiment rhubarbe et concombre

Mackerel tartare with a rhubarb and cucumber relish

Mackerel makes a wonderful alternative to the classic salmon *tartare* seen on French bistro menus. Cucumber adds a crunch factor and the acidic note of the raw rhubarb cuts through the oiliness of the fish. Don't worry about eating raw rhubarb. It's the leaves that are poisonous, not the stalks.

• 4 mackerel fillets, skinned* • a pinch of salt
• 1 tablespoon extra virgin olive oil, plus extra for drizzling

For the relish • 1 stick of rhubarb, finely diced
• 1 small cucumber, finely diced • 1 tablespoon freshly squeezed lemon juice
• 1 tablespoon cider vinegar • a pinch of salt • 1 teaspoon sugar, or to taste

Make the relish by mixing all the ingredients together. Leave to stand for 10 minutes.

Meanwhile, check the fish for any bones before cutting into very small dice. Put the diced fish into a bowl, season with the salt and olive oil, and mix together. Serve immediately, with the relish and a drizzle of olive oil.

* *It's essential to use the freshest mackerel possible. I buy my mackerel whole so that I can see how fresh the fish is. Here are a few tips on how to tell whether fish is fresh:*
  * *Bright, shiny eyes*
  * *Glossy skin*
  * *It doesn't smell 'fishy'*
  * *If you look under the gills, they should be a rich red. Faded, dull red means the fish is old.*

Preparation time: 20 minutes

Steak tartare

Steak tartare

There's honestly not much to making *steak tartare*. A good-quality fillet of beef, minced or chopped, with some condiments: *c'est tout!*

Some bistros serve their *tartares* already seasoned and with the condiments mixed into the meat. I prefer the easier option of just serving the condiments on the side. This way, everyone can customize their *tartare* to their own taste.

• 800g very fresh beef fillet, minced or finely chopped by hand • 4 fresh egg yolks*
• pepper (optional) • 4 tablespoons capers, finely chopped • 2 shallots, finely chopped
• 8 *cornichons*, finely chopped • ½ bunch of parsley, finely chopped • Dijon mustard
• Tabasco • Worcestershire sauce

Divide the beef between 4 plates, using your hands to form the meat into patties. Top each *tartare* with an egg yolk, and sprinkle with pepper if you like. Put the chopped condiments into little bowls, and pop the mustard, Tabasco and Worcestershire sauce on the table for everyone to help themselves. Serve with some crusty bread.

* This classic steak tartare is served with a raw egg yolk, but I prefer mine without as I find the egg too rich with the meat.

Japanese twist

Try the following Japanese accompaniments instead of the classic condiments above.

• 1 tablespoon sugar • 5 tablespoons rice wine vinegar • 1 small cucumber, cut into very small cubes
• 2 *daikon* (white radishes), about 20cm long, cut into very small cubes

Dissolve the sugar in the rice wine vinegar. Stir in the cucumber and radish. Leave to marinate for 30 minutes, stirring occasionally. Serve with some pickled Japanese ginger and a small dab of wasabi paste.

Preparation time: 10–15 minutes
Resting time: 30 minutes (for the Japanese condiment)

Bouillon de poulet avec des quenelles de volailles

Chicken dumpling soup

Soup for your soul, or for when you're ill. My Austrian grandma used to make a chicken dumpling soup that I always crave when I'm feeling a little under the weather. Dumplings (or *quenelles* in French) are traditionally served with a heavy sauce, but I think they go just as well in this light soup.

• 1.5 litres chicken stock • 2 large carrots, roughly chopped
• 5 button mushrooms, thinly sliced • salt and pepper (if needed)*
• ½ bunch of parsley, leaves roughly chopped

For the quenelles • 200g raw chicken breast • 100g white bread, no crusts • 100ml single cream
• 1 egg plus 1 egg yolk • 1 teaspoon salt • a pinch of pepper • a pinch of nutmeg

Put the stock and carrots into a large pot. Bring the stock to a boil and boil for 10 minutes.

Meanwhile, put all the ingredients for the *quenelles* into an electric blender and whizz until you have a smooth paste. Form the paste into 20–25 *quenelle* shapes by using 2 tablespoons (for smaller *quenelles*, use 2 teaspoons). Drop the *quenelles* into the boiling stock and cook for 5 minutes (3 minutes for the small ones), adding the mushrooms for the last minute. When the *quenelles* are done, they will rise to the surface. Serve immediately, garnished with some roughly chopped parsley.

*Depending on the quality of your stock, you may not need to add any salt or pepper. Taste for seasoning before serving.

The traditional way with *quenelles*

Poach the *quenelles* in boiling water until they rise to the surface, then drain and put into a baking dish. Cover with grated cheese or *Sauce Béchamel* (see page 269) and grill until the top is bubbling and golden.

Preparation time: 30 minutes   Cooking time: 20 minutes

Navarin d'agneau printanier

Spring lamb stew

For the fashion-conscious, the arrival of spring in Paris means that it's out with the winter wardrobe and in with the spring one. The same goes for stews. Forget your winter *boeuf bourguignon*, it's so last season! *Navarin printanier*, a lamb stew with fresh spring vegetables, is what should be bubbling away in your kitchen.

• 1kg lamb neck, cut into 6 pieces • 2 cloves of garlic, crushed to a paste • 1 onion, finely chopped • 1 tablespoon olive oil • 1 bay leaf • 2 sprigs of thyme • 4 carrots, cut into chunks • 100g fresh or frozen peas • 100g green beans, chopped • salt and pepper

Preheat the oven to 160°C. Brown the meat, garlic and onion with the olive oil in a large flameproof casserole (*cocotte*). Add the bay leaf, thyme and carrots, and enough water to cover the meat by at least a couple of centimetres. Bring to a simmer and remove any scum that rises to the top. Once all the scum is removed, cover the pan and transfer to the oven. Cook for 1½–2 hours or until the meat is tender.

Ten minutes before serving, bring a large pot of salted water to a boil and add the peas and beans. Cook for 5 minutes or until the vegetables are tender, then drain.

Take the casserole out of the oven and remove the bay leaf and sprigs of thyme. Add the peas and beans to the lamb with salt and pepper to taste, and serve straight away.

For an English twist
Serve the stew with some mint sauce.

Preparation time: 30 minutes Cooking time: 1½–2 hours

Hachis Parmentier tricolore

Three-coloured 'shepherd's pie'

I thought *Hachis Parmentier* was a French take on English shepherd's pie until I realized it doesn't use mince but leftover meat from a stew or roast. Antoine-Augustin Parmentier was an eighteenth-century French pharmacist who championed the humble potato. Previously used as animal fodder, Parmentier put potatoes on the French culinary map by promoting them as a nutritious vegetable at high-society banquets and dinners. *Hachis Parmentier* with its mashed-potato topping is an *hommage* to the man who made potatoes fashionable. This is my colourful version.

• 3 shallots, thinly sliced • 2 cloves of garlic, crushed to a paste • 1 carrot, finely diced
• 1 bay leaf • 1 sprig of thyme (leaves only) • 1 tablespoon olive oil • 2 tablespoons tomato paste
• 300g roast or stewed meat,* shredded • 100ml vegetable stock, plus a little extra if needed
• a pinch of sugar • salt and pepper

For the topping • 500g pumpkin, peeled and cut into chunks • olive oil
• 500g floury potatoes, e.g. Desirée or King Edward • salt • ½ bunch of parsley
• 8 tablespoons milk • 1 tablespoon butter • nutmeg • white pepper

Preheat the oven to 200°C. Toss the pumpkin chunks into a large roasting tray and drizzle with olive oil. Roast for 20 minutes or until tender. Whizz to a smooth paste in the blender, then season to taste with nutmeg and salt. Spoon into a piping bag or a heavy-duty food bag.

Cook the potatoes in a large pot of boiling salted water for 15–20 minutes or until tender. In an electric blender, whizz the parsley (including the stalks) with 3 tablespoons olive oil until smooth. Once the potatoes are cooked, drain and mash until smooth with the milk and butter. Season with nutmeg, salt and white pepper. Split into 2 equal portions and mix the parsley paste into one. Spoon each portion of mash into a piping bag or heavy-duty food bag.

Fry the shallots, garlic, carrot, bay leaf and thyme with the olive oil until the shallots are translucent and soft. Add the tomato paste, meat, stock, sugar, salt and pepper, and cook for a further 5 minutes.

To assemble, pour the meat mixture into a large baking dish and cover with piped lines of the different toppings. (If you're using food bags for the piping, cut a corner off each bag and squeeze the mash out at the corner.) Bake for 30 minutes or until bubbling and golden. Serve hot.

* You could use leftovers from a Pot-au-feu *(see page 199).*

Preparation time: 45 minutes Cooking time: 1 hour

Boulettes de viande avec une sauce piquante et des pâtes d'Alsace

Meatballs in spicy sauce with Alsatian pasta

Pasta is not what comes to mind when you think of French food, but Alsace (the French region bordering Germany) is renowned for its egg pasta. Most pasta is made of hard wheat flour and water, whereas Alsatian pasta is made from hard wheat flour and fresh eggs.

• 400g pasta, preferably Alsatian egg pasta • 250g sausagemeat (or sausage with casings removed)
• 250g minced beef • 1 tablespoon olive oil • chopped parsley, to garnish

For the spicy sauce* • 500ml veal or beef stock, warm • 30g butter • 30g plain flour
• 30g *lardons* or cubes of smoked bacon • 1 onion, finely chopped • 1 carrot, finely chopped
• 1 stick of celery, finely chopped • 1 tablespoon tomato paste • 175ml red wine
• 1 bouquet garni (thyme, bay leaf, parsley stalks, peppercorns)
• 2 tablespoons *cornichons*, finely chopped • 2 tablespoons capers, finely chopped

To make the sauce, fry the vegetables and *lardons* on a medium heat until golden. Remove them from the pan with a slotted spoon, then add the butter. Melt over a medium heat, sprinkle in the flour and stir constantly until it turns an almost Coca-Cola colour. Turn the heat down to low and slowly pour in the warm stock, whisking energetically. Add the tomato paste and wine and whisk until the paste has dissolved. Pop the fried vegetables and *lardons* back into the pan, add the bouquet garni and simmer gently for 15 minutes. Pour the sauce through a sieve and add the chopped *cornichons* and capers. Taste for seasoning and set aside until needed.**

Meanwhile, make the meatballs. Mix together the minced beef and sausagemeat. Form balls slightly smaller than a golf ball. Fry in a large non-stick frying pan with the olive oil for about 5 minutes or until cooked through. Pour the sauce over the meatballs, stir together and heat through.

Cook the pasta according to packet instructions. Drain and serve with the meatballs in the sauce, sprinkled with a little chopped parsley.

* You can make a creamy sauce instead, by simply adding 2 tablespoons each finely chopped cornichons *and* capers *to Sauce Béchamel (see page 269). It goes just as well with the meatballs as the spicy sauce.*

** The sauce (without the capers and cornichons*) will keep for several days in an airtight container in the fridge, and it can also be frozen.*

Preparation time: 30 minutes   Cooking time: 30 minutes

Saucisse et purée de pomme de terre avec une sauce diable

Bangers 'n' mash with devil's gravy

My butcher makes great sausages. The perfect way to serve them? With mashed potatoes and gravy, in this case *sauce diable*, an *espagnole* sauce with white wine, shallots and cayenne pepper.

• a knob of butter • 4 shallots, finely sliced • 8 sausages

For the sauce diable • 1 onion, finely chopped • 1 carrot, finely chopped
• 1 stick of celery, finely chopped • 30g *lardons* or cubes of smoked bacon • 30g butter
• 30g plain flour • 500ml veal or beef stock, warm • 1 tablespoon tomato paste
• 175ml dry white wine • 1 bouquet garni (thyme, bay leaf, parsley stalks, peppercorns)
• a pinch of cayenne pepper

For the mash • 700g floury potatoes (e.g. Maris Piper or King Edward), peeled
• 2 knobs of butter • 100–200ml milk, lukewarm • nutmeg • salt

Put the potatoes on to boil in salted water for 15–20 minutes until tender.

To make the sauce, fry the vegetables and *lardons* on a medium heat until golden. Remove them from the pan (try and keep as much of the fat as possible in the pan), then add the butter. Melt over a medium heat, sprinkle in the flour and stir constantly until it turns an almost Coca-Cola colour. Turn the heat down to low and slowly pour in the warm stock, whisking energetically. Add the tomato paste and wine and whisk until the paste has dissolved. Pop the fried vegetables and *lardons* back into the pan, add the bouquet garni and simmer gently for 15 minutes. Pour the sauce through a sieve, add the cayenne and taste for seasoning. Set aside until needed.*

Meanwhile, melt the butter in a large non-stick frying pan and fry the shallots until soft. Add the shallots to the sauce and use the same pan to fry the sausages for 6–8 minutes or until cooked through. Turn them occasionally so that they become evenly browned on all sides.

Drain the potatoes, put back into the pan and heat, stirring constantly, until dry. Once the potatoes have stopped steaming, push them through a potato ricer or Mouli. Mix with the butter and add enough warm milk to make a smooth, creamy mash. Season with nutmeg and a little salt.

To serve, reheat the sauce and pour over the sausages and mash.

The sauce will keep for several days in an airtight container in the fridge, and it can also be frozen.

Preparation time: 30 minutes Cooking time: 45–50 minutes

LA POMME
 LE SAC À DOS
 LES OEUFS
 LE CAHIER
 LA TABLE
 LE CHOCOLAT

 LE FOUR
 LA LIMONADE
 LA CASSEROLE
 LES CRAYONS
 LA FRAMBOISE
 L'ASSIETTE

 LE SANDWICH

 LE GÂTEAU

Snack Time

Le goûter

 LE CITRON

 LES OEUFS

 LA TABLE

 LE SAC À DOS

 LE CAHIER
 LA CASSEROLE
 LA POMME
 LE FOUR
 LE ROBINET
 LE SANDWICH

 LE CHOCOLAT
 L'ASSIETTE
 LE CITRON
 LA FRAMBOISE
 LA LIMONADE
 LES CRAYONS

Snacking between meals is not really the done thing in France. Even French food adverts come with a slogan: 'Pour être en forme, évitez de grignoter dans la journée' ('to stay in shape, avoid snacking during the day'). However, le goûter is an exception. Similar to the British 'afternoon tea', it's a little less formal – no cream teas with scones here. A simple sweet or savoury snack around 4 p.m. lets the French 'avoir la pêche' ('have the peach', or be in great form).

My first job in Paris taught me a thing or two about the way of life in the city of lights. Working for a French–Scottish family, looking after two girls, gave me a great insight. They were more than happy to show me the French way of doing things and I quickly learned that le goûter is an essential part of daily life, especially for French kids. Mothers, grandmothers and nannies would be waiting at the school gates with a snack in hand or would pop by the local boulangerie to pick one up.

Le goûter is not just for kids, though; adults need their afternoon pick-me-up too! I love all the recipes in this chapter, but a particular favourite snack has to be a simple pain au chocolat – not the flaky croissant type more usually eaten for breakfast but, quite simply, a piece of bread (fresh crusty baguette works best) stuffed with a piece of good-quality chocolate (dark or milk, follow your tastebuds, it doesn't really matter). This is something I came across during my time as a nanny and it's probably not the healthiest snack, but then le goûter is also about indulging oneself a little. And the French are the absolute masters at that . . .

Croque Madame muffins

Cheese, ham and egg sandwich muffins

Croque Monsieur is essentially a toasted cheese and ham sandwich. Put a fried egg on top and you've got a *Croque Madame* (the egg is supposed to resemble a lady's hat). What makes the difference between a toasted cheese and ham sandwich and a *Croque Monsieur* is the cheese – in a *Croque Monsieur* it comes in the form of a creamy cheese sauce. And boy, does this make a difference!

My version of *Croque Madame* uses the bread as a muffin cup to contain the delicious cheese sauce and egg. Great as a snack, or have it with a green salad and fries, as they serve it in French cafés.

• 6 large slices of white bread, no crusts • 3 tablespoons butter, melted
• 75g ham, cut into cubes or thin strips • 6 small eggs

For the Mornay (cheese) sauce • 1 tablespoon butter • 1 tablespoon plain flour
• 200ml milk, lukewarm • ½ teaspoon Dijon mustard • ½ teaspoon nutmeg
• 30g Gruyère or mature Comté cheese (or a strong hard cheese like Parmesan or mature Cheddar), grated • salt and pepper

To make the sauce, melt the butter in a pan over a medium heat. Add the flour and beat hard until you have a smooth paste. Take off the heat and leave to cool for 2 minutes, then gradually add the milk, whisking constantly. Place the pan back over a medium heat, add the mustard and nutmeg and simmer gently for 10 minutes, whisking frequently to stop the sauce burning on the bottom of the pan. Once the sauce thickens and has the consistency of a thick tomato sauce, take it off the heat. Add the cheese (keep a little for the garnish) and taste for seasoning. If the sauce is too thick, add a little more milk. If it's lumpy, pass it through a sieve.

To assemble, preheat the oven to 180°C. Flatten the slices of bread with a rolling pin, then brush each slice on both sides with melted butter. Line a 6-hole muffin tin with the slices of bread, pressing them in with the bottom of a small glass. Divide the ham between the muffins followed by the eggs (if the egg seems too big, pour a little of the white away before using). Put 2 tablespoons cheese sauce on top of each egg, then sprinkle with a little cheese and pepper. Bake for 15–20 minutes, depending on how runny you like your eggs. Serve immediately.

Preparation time: 20 minutes Baking time: 15–20 minutes

Crêpes et galettes

Pancakes and buckwheat pancakes

The Americans have burgers and hotdogs, the English sandwiches. The French? They have *crêpes* and *galettes*. Originally from Brittany, they have been adopted as the national snack, and tiny booths serving hot discs of doughy goodness can be found on virtually every Parisian street (or so it seems). Order a *crêpe* with a simple sprinkle of sugar, or choose from a list of fillings such as chocolate spread or *crème de marrons* (sweetened chestnut cream) – or try egg, cheese and ham in a buckwheat pancake. If you're eating them the traditional way, they should be washed down with a glass of Breton cider. See page 78 for some filling and topping ideas.

For the crêpes • 200g plain flour • a pinch of sugar • a pinch of salt
• 2 eggs • about 600ml milk • melted butter, for frying

For the galettes • 200g buckwheat flour • a pinch of salt
• about 600ml water • melted butter, for frying

To make the *crêpes*, mix the flour, sugar and salt in a bowl. Make a well in the centre and crack in the eggs. Gradually mix the ingredients together, adding enough milk for the batter to have the consistency of double cream. Don't overmix as this will make rubbery *crêpes*. Refrigerate for a minimum of an hour, or overnight.

Heat a 15–18cm *crêpe* pan and brush with some melted butter. Stir the batter and add more milk if necessary to give it the consistency of double cream (it may have thickened on standing). Pour 50–60ml of the batter into the pan and quickly swirl the pan so the batter covers the whole of the inside. Cook for 1 minute, loosen around the edge with a spatula, then turn the *crêpe* over and cook for a further minute. Slide the *crêpe* out of the pan*, then repeat to make 10–12 *crêpes* altogether, greasing the pan with butter in between each one.**

To make the *galettes*, mix the flour and salt in a bowl. Make a well in the centre and gradually mix in the water, adding only enough for the batter to have the consistency of double cream. Don't overmix as this will make rubbery *galettes*. Refrigerate for a minimum of an hour, or overnight. Before using, whisk again and add more water if necessary. Cook the same way as the *crêpes*.

* *Don't worry – the first one always tends to come out a little wrong.*

** *To keep the cooked* crêpes/galettes *warm: place them on a baking tray, cover loosely with aluminium foil and place in the oven at 120°C.*

Preparation time: 10 minutes Resting time: 1 hour–overnight
Cooking time: 30 minutes

Filling and topping ideas for *crêpes* and *galettes*

To be honest, you could pretty much serve anything with a *crêpe* or *galette*, as long as it's not too liquid. Here are some ideas.

Sweet: sugar and lemon, chocolate spread, jam, *crème fraîche* or whipped cream with fresh fruit (especially berries), caramel spread, ice cream.

Savoury: cheese, ham or other cooked meats, leftover roast meat, smoked salmon, salad, tomatoes, fried egg, roasted vegetables, mushrooms.

Crêpes avec une sauce Suzette caramelisée

Pancakes with a caramel Suzette sauce

• finely grated zest of 1 unwaxed orange • juice of 2 oranges (about 150ml)
• 75ml orange liqueur • 100g sugar • 100g soft butter, cubed • 10–12 *Crêpes* (see page 77)

Put the orange zest and juice into a pan with the liqueur and sugar. Reduce for 15 minutes or until you have a thick, golden syrup*. Whisk in a cube of butter at a time, taking care as the hot caramel may splutter.

Fold the warm *crepes* into quarters and place on a serving dish. Pour the sauce over the *crepes* and serve immediately.

* If you prefer the traditional crêpe Suzette *sauce, just bring the orange zest and juice, liqueur and sugar to a boil (don't caramelize), then turn off the heat and whisk in the butter.*

Preparation time: 5 minutes Cooking time: 15 minutes

LANGERIE

LA FARINE DE MEULE

DE CHAUSSONS

POMMES FRAÎCHES

Tartines sucrées et salées

Sweet and savoury open-faced sandwiches

Tartine comes from the French verb *tartiner*, meaning to spread. You *tartine* your topping on to a slice of bread or toast, making an open sandwich. Whether it's the classic butter and jam for breakfast or the after-school children's favourite of chocolate squares, *tartine* toppings should remain simple and the bread is just as important as what goes on top – if not more so. Choosing bread in a *boulangerie* can be quite overwhelming. Of course there's the classic *baguette,* but then there's a whole range of other breads such as sourdough, wholegrain and rye, and breads with nuts, figs and other dried fruit. *Tartines* are all about enjoying the simple pleasure of a good piece of bread or toast with a topping or two.

Each topping is enough for one piece of bread or toast.

Savoury toppings

Roast ham and pear
Brush the bread or toast with a little extra virgin olive oil. Thinly slice half a pear. Top the bread with the pear and some strips of roast ham.

Radish and salted butter
Spread the bread or toast with some salted butter (alternatively mix 1 tablespoon unsalted butter with some coarse sea salt). Thinly slice several radishes and place on top.

Avocado and grapefruit
Slice half an avocado. Cut out the segments from a quarter of a grapefruit. Arrange the avocado and grapefruit on the bread or toast. Sprinkle with a little salt and olive oil.

Goat's cheese, fig and walnuts
Cut a fig into thin slices and place on the bread. Crumble some goat's cheese on top, followed by a couple of walnuts. Put under the grill for a minute or two if you like.

Sweet toppings

Caramelized apples

Butter the bread with some salted butter. Thinly slice half a small apple. Arrange the apple slices on the bread and sprinkle with sugar. Set under the grill for a couple of minutes until caramelized, or use a blow torch to caramelize the sugar. Works equally well with other fruit such as bananas, plums and pears.

Strawberries, *crème fraîche* and mint

Spread a generous layer of *crème fraîche* over the bread or toast. Top with sliced strawberries, a few leaves of mint, a sprinkle of sugar and a little more *crème fraîche*.

Chocolate and olive oil

Put a chocolate bar into the freezer for 10 minutes before grating a generous handful. Brush the bread with some extra virgin olive oil and top with the grated chocolate. Put under the grill for a couple of minutes for a melted chocolate tartine.

Peach and Brie

Thinly slice half a peach. Top the bread or toast with a few slices of the peach and some Brie cheese.

Chouquettes

Sugar puffs

Light, airy puffs covered with nibbed sugar (coarse sugar that doesn't melt), *chouquettes* are less well known than *profiteroles* and *éclairs*, their choux-pastry cousins. *Chouquette* is derived from *chou* (cabbage), and the French use the endearing expression *mon petit chou* for their loved ones. 'My little cabbage' doesn't have quite the same ring in English, though, does it? Make sure you have all your ingredients measured and ready to hand.

• 125ml water • 125ml milk • 100g butter, cubed • 1 teaspoon salt
• 1 teaspoon sugar • 170g strong plain flour* • 4 eggs • icing sugar, for dusting
• 100g nibbed sugar (also called pearl or hail sugar)**

Preheat the oven to 180°C. Pour the water and milk into a pan and add the butter, salt and sugar. Place the pan on a high heat and melt the butter. Turn the heat down to low and add all of the flour. Beat hard. At this point the mixture will have the consistency of lumpy mashed potatoes. Continue beating until you have a smooth ball that pulls away from the sides of the pan without sticking.

Take the pan off the heat and continue to beat until the dough is cold enough to touch. Mix in the eggs one at a time – the batter will go lumpy when you add them, but beating continuously will smooth it out. Once all the eggs are incorporated and the mixture is smooth, put the dough into a piping bag fitted with a 5mm nozzle. Line several baking trays with baking paper, dotting a little dough in each corner to stick the paper down.

To pipe the *chouquettes*, hold the nozzle at a 90° degree angle about 5mm from the tray. Keep the nozzle upright and pipe a walnut-sized ball of dough, then quickly flick the nozzle sideways to stop the dough trailing. Repeat to make 20–30 *chouquettes*, with a 2cm gap between. If they come out too pointy, dip your finger in some water and gently pat the points down, otherwise they will burn in the oven.

Dust the *chouquettes* with icing sugar and then leave for a minute before sprinkling with the nibbed sugar. Repeat with a second layer of icing sugar before baking for 20 minutes or until golden and crisp.

Chouquettes are best eaten straight away, but they can be kept in an airtight container for several days. To crisp up, bake at 150°C for 5 minutes.

* For chocolate choux pastry, replace 20g flour with 20g unsweetened cocoa powder.

** Instead of nibbed sugar, try finely chopped nuts mixed with a little raw cane sugar, or chocolate chips.

Preparation time: 30 minutes Baking time: 20–30 minutes

Gougères

Cheese puffs

The savoury version of *chouquettes* (see page 84). They are traditionally sprinkled with a strong cheese, like a mature Comté, but I like them topped with black sesame seeds, herbs and spices too. These savoury, salty puffs are seriously moreish. Make sure you have all your ingredients measured and ready to hand.

- 125ml water • 125ml milk • 100g butter, cubed • 1 teaspoon salt
- 1 teaspoon sugar • a pinch of chilli powder • 170g strong plain flour
- 75g mature hard or semi-hard cheese (e.g. Gruyère, Comté, Parmesan or Cheddar), grated
- 2 tablespoons finely chopped herbs, e.g. parsley, coriander, basil or chives (optional) • 4 eggs

Preheat the oven to 180°C. Pour the water and milk into a pan and add the butter, salt, sugar and chilli powder. Place the pan on a high heat and melt the butter. Turn the heat down to low and add all of the flour. Beat hard. At this point the mixture will have the consistency of lumpy mashed potatoes. Add 50g of the grated cheese and then the chopped herbs (if using). Continue beating until you have a smooth paste that does not stick to the sides of the pan.

Take the pan off the heat and continue to beat until the pastry is cold enough to touch. Mix in the eggs one at the time. The batter will go lumpy when you add them, but beating continuously will smooth it out. Once all the eggs are incorporated and the mixture is smooth, put the dough into a piping bag fitted with a 5mm nozzle. Line several baking trays with baking paper, dotting a little dough in each corner to stick down the paper.

To pipe the *gougères*, hold the nozzle at a 90° degree angle about 5mm from the tray. Keep the nozzle upright and pipe a walnut-sized ball of dough, then quickly flick the nozzle sideways to stop the dough trailing. Repeat to make 20–30 *gougères*, leaving a 2cm gap between each one. If they come out too pointy in shape, dip your finger in some water and gently pat the points down, otherwise they will burn in the oven. Sprinkle with the rest of the grated cheese* before baking for 20 minutes or until golden and crisp.

Gougères are best eaten straight away, but they can be kept in an airtight container for several days. To crisp up, bake at 150°C for 5 minutes.

* *Instead of the cheese topping, you could have a sprinkling of poppy, nigella, caraway or sesame seeds, or you could top the* gougères *with both the cheese and the seeds.*

Preparation time: 30 minutes Baking time: 20 minutes

Madeleines à la crème au citron

Madeleines with lemon curd

This recipe was given to me by my friend Frankie Unsworth who, like me, studied *pâtisserie* at Le Cordon Bleu in Paris. Frankie says, 'The lemon curd may take its inspiration from Melbourne's Cumulus Inc., but the basic recipe harks back to our Cordon Bleu days, when Rachel and I learned how to make this *goûter* treat. The batter can be made in advance, then baked in time for tea – madeleines should always be eaten fresh from the oven.'

• 3 eggs • 130g sugar • 200g plain flour
• 10g baking powder • finely grated zest of 1 unwaxed lemon • 20g honey
• 60ml milk • 200g butter, melted and cooled • a punnet of raspberries • icing sugar, for dusting

For the lemon curd • finely grated zest and juice of 1 unwaxed lemon
• a pinch of salt • 40g sugar • 45g butter • 2 egg yolks

Beat the eggs with the sugar until pale and frothy. Measure the flour and baking powder into a separate bowl and add the lemon zest. Mix the honey and milk with the cool butter, then add to the eggs. In 2 batches, fold in the flour. Cover and leave to rest in the fridge for a few hours, or overnight.

Meanwhile, make the lemon curd. Put the lemon zest and juice, salt, sugar and butter into a small saucepan and heat gently until the sugar and butter have melted. Remove from the heat. Whisk the egg yolks in a bowl, then add to the pan and whisk vigorously. Return the pan to a low heat and whisk constantly as the curd starts to thicken. Don't stop whisking or the eggs will curdle (if the curd starts to boil, take off the heat). Once the curd thickens and releases a bubble or two, remove from the heat and pass the curd through a sieve into a bowl. Place cling film in direct contact with the curd and refrigerate for at least an hour, preferably overnight.

When you are ready to bake, preheat the oven to 190°C. Butter and flour a 12-shell madeleine tin. Put the lemon curd into a piping bag fitted with a small, pointed nozzle and place in the fridge.

Put a heaped tablespoon of batter into each madeleine shell and press a raspberry deep into the batter. Bake for 5 minutes, turn the oven off for 1 minute (the madeleines will get their signature peaks), then turn the oven on to 160°C and bake for a further 5 minutes. Transfer the madeleines to a wire rack and leave for a few minutes until cool enough to handle. Meanwhile, wash and dry the tin, then repeat the baking as for the first batch. While the second batch is baking, pop the piping nozzle into the mound in each baked madeleine and squirt in a teaspoon's worth of lemon curd. Repeat with the second batch, then dust with icing sugar and serve straight away.

Preparation time: 40 minutes Resting time: a few hours–overnight
Cooking time: 15 minutes Baking time: 22 minutes

Quatre-quarts aux agrumes

Citrus fruit cake

Quatre-quarts is the French equivalent of the English sponge cake. It's a recipe that most French cooks know off by heart because it's so simple to remember. As its name suggests, it has four main ingredients (flour, sugar, eggs and butter) in equal measures. *C'est tout!*

• 4 eggs • 250g golden caster sugar • 250g plain flour • a pinch of salt
• finely grated zest of 1 unwaxed lemon and 1 unwaxed orange
• 1 teaspoon baking powder • 250g butter, melted and cooled

Preheat the oven to 180°C and butter and flour a 23 x 12cm loaf tin. Separate the eggs. In a bowl, beat the egg whites to stiff peaks with half of the sugar. In another bowl, beat the egg yolks and the other half of the sugar until thick and pale in colour.

In a separate bowl, mix the flour, salt, zest and baking powder together.

Fold the flour mixture into the egg yolk mixture, then pour in the melted and cooled butter, stirring gently until the butter is just incorporated into the mix. Finally, carefully fold in the egg whites.

Pour the batter into the prepared tin, then bake for 35–40 minutes or until the point of a knife comes out clean when inserted in the centre.

The cake is best eaten the same day, but it will keep in an airtight container for a day or two.

Preparation time: 20 minutes   Baking time: 35–40 minutes

Briochettes au dulce de leche

Dulce de leche brioche buns

The *brioche* recipe I use here is similar to *brioche vendéenne*, which is traditionally shaped as a plait for Easter and is made with *crème fraîche* and orange flower water.

The dough makes a great base for buns, and one of my favourite fillings is the Argentinian caramel spread *dulce de leche*. I discovered it during my first cooking job in Paris, at the cookery store La Cocotte. I used to bake *coquetines* (biscuits filled with *dulce de leche*) and other sweet treats for their tea salon and book events.

• 75g butter • 50ml milk • 5g dried yeast • 250g plain flour • 50g sugar • a pinch of salt
• 1 egg, beaten • 1 heaped tablespoon *crème fraîche* • 1 teaspoon vanilla extract
• 1 teaspoon orange flower water • beaten egg, for the eggwash

For the filling • 150g *dulce de leche*

For the optional filling • 3 small dessert apples, cored and roughly chopped, or 150g nuts
(e.g. almonds or hazelnuts), roughly chopped

Melt the butter in the milk. Add the yeast and stir to dissolve (the milk should be lukewarm, definitely not hot, otherwise the yeast will not work).

In a large bowl, mix together the flour, sugar and salt. Create a well in the middle, add the milk mixture and the rest of the ingredients, and combine together until you have a soft, sticky dough. Place in a bowl, cover with cling film and refrigerate overnight.

The next day, line a 25cm springform tin (8–10cm deep), or a regular cake tin, with baking paper. Turn the dough on to a well-floured surface and knead for 5 minutes, then roll into a large rectangle (roughly 40 x 30cm). Spread the *dulce de leche* on top, leaving a 2cm border, and sprinkle over the chopped apples or nuts (if using). Roll up the dough to make a long sausage and cut into 6 equal pieces. Place each piece, swirl-side up, into the prepared tin and brush with eggwash. Cover and leave to rise in a warm place for 2 hours or until doubled in size.

Preheat the oven to 160°C. Eggwash the buns a second time and then bake for 30–40 minutes or until golden brown. If the *briochettes* start browning too much, cover with some aluminium foil. Remove from the oven and transfer to a wire rack to cool. Best eaten warm, or on the same day.

Preparation time: 30 minutes
Resting time: overnight, plus a couple of hours
Baking time: 30–40 minutes

Pain perdu avec compote de cerises et basilic

French toast with cherry and basil compote

Pain perdu means 'lost bread', but this dish finds its way to my stomach quite easily. I've topped it with my favourite compote, but you can eat it just as it comes, without any topping at all.

• 1 egg • 250ml milk • 1 tablespoon sugar
• 4 slices of *brioche* or sandwich bread • 1 tablespoon butter

For the compote* • 450g frozen pitted cherries • 150g icing sugar • a bunch of basil (about 20g)

To make the compote, place all the ingredients in a pot and simmer uncovered for 15 minutes. Stir occasionally during this time to help dissolve the icing sugar.

Meanwhile, make the *pain perdu*. Whisk the egg, milk and sugar together in a dish. Place the *brioche* in the egg mixture and soak for a minute on each side. Heat the butter in a large frying pan on a medium heat. Add the *brioche* and cook for 2–3 minutes or until golden, then flip the slices over and cook the other side.

Remove the basil from the compote. Serve the *pain perdu* straight from the pan, with the warm compote spooned over and around.

*The compote can be made in advance and kept for several days in an airtight container in the fridge, ready to be reheated when you want it.

Other topping ideas

• *sliced banana and chocolate sauce*
• *crispy bacon and maple syrup*
• *fresh berries and a scoop of ice cream*
• *salted caramel sauce (see page 249).*

Preparation time: 10 minutes Cooking time: 25 minutes

Fromage frais

Fresh cheese

Fromage frais has a smooth, creamy taste and a subtle acidic note, making it less smelly socks and more freshly washed white linen. Of course, an additional plus is that it's low in fat and cholesterol, but that doesn't mean it's low in taste.

- 2 litres fresh semi-skimmed or skimmed milk, preferably organic but not UHT or homogenized
- 125g plain live or probiotic yoghurt, preferably organic, • juice of 1 lemon (6 tablespoons)
- a pinch of salt or sugar • 2 tablespoons double cream (optional)

Pour the milk into a large pot. Heat very slowly, stirring gently, until it starts to steam and little bubbles form around the edge (it should not boil at any point). This should take about 20 minutes.

Allow to cool for a couple of minutes before stirring in the yoghurt and lemon juice. Leave to sit undisturbed for a further 10 minutes. Return the pot to the heat and bring the milk to a boil. Once it separates into curds (the solids) and whey (the liquid), remove from the heat.

Line a fine-meshed sieve with cheesecloth or a clean tea towel. Place the sieve over a bowl and pour in the separated milk. Scrunch the cloth tightly immediately above the cheese, like making a money bag, and twist to squeeze out any excess liquid. Now tie the corners of the cloth together to form a hanging pouch and thread a wooden spoon through the loop. Hang the cheese over a large bowl or jug (don't let it sit on the bottom), and refrigerate for 30 minutes or overnight. The longer the cheese hangs, the more the liquid will drip away and the drier the cheese will become.

To serve, twist the cloth as before to squeeze out any excess liquid, then remove the cheese from the cloth and season with salt or sugar. Serve as it comes for a firm version, or beat in a couple of tablespoons of double cream for a smoother, creamier cheese.

Serving ideas

Spread the cheese over a slice of toasted *brioche* or bread, then just let your imagination and tastebuds get creative to sweeten or spice it up. These are some of my favourite flavourings.

Sweet: a drizzle of honey, maple syrup or a sprinkling of sugar can be quite sufficient. Or serve with fresh or stewed fruit (berries are especially good). For a crunch factor, try nuts or granola.

Savoury: cracked black pepper, a pinch of chilli, or freshly chopped herbs (chives, parsley, etc.).

Preparation time: 10 minutes   Cooking time: 25 minutes
Resting time: 30 minutes–overnight

LE SOLEIL

LE SAUCISSON SEC

LA BAGUETTE

L'HERBE

LES VERRES

UNE BOUTEILLE
DE VIN

LA PLUIE

LES FROMAGES

LES RAISINS

LE THERMOS

LES SERVIETTES

LA COUVERTURE

LE PANIER

Summer Picnics

Pique-niques d'été

LE THERMOS

LA PLUIE

L'ARBRE

LE SAUCISSON SEC

LES VERRES

L'HERBE

LE TIRE-BOUCHON

LA COUVERTURE

LE SOLEIL

UNE BOUTEILLE
DE VIN

LES ABEILLES

LA BAGUETTE

LES FROMAGES

LE PANIER

LES RAISINS

LES FLEURS

In the mid-nineteenth century, Édouard Manet and Claude Monet both painted picnic scenes, *Le déjeuner sur l'herbe* ('lunch on the grass'). Manet's painting (which in turn inspired Monet) caused quite a stir. The picnic is set in a luscious green opening in a forest. A naked woman sits with two fully dressed men, who are so deep in conversation that they don't seem at all distracted by their nude companion. Fruits and bread seem to have spilled out of their picnic basket, but none of the guests seems to be too bothered about eating. That is certainly not the case with the Parisian picnics I've been to – the food is the star of the show!

In Paris, as soon as spring sunshine begins to warm the city and cold, grey winter weather is chased away, you'll find Parisians heading to any green or watery spot. Along the Seine or the canal, on the Champ de Mars under the Eiffel Tower and in many other Parisian parks, people congregate with their baguettes, bottles of wine and other picnic paraphernalia.

My favourite park in Paris has to be the Parc des Buttes Chaumont in the 19th arrondissement. Unlike the Jardin du Luxembourg or Parc Monceau, this park is very green, with plenty of grass that you can actually sit on (whereas some Parisian parks ban sitting on the grass), lots of trees and a beautiful view over Paris. During the summer months it becomes my second home, especially since I'm lucky enough to live next door. Picnics are *the* summer social gatherings amongst my friends, as we all have typical tiny Parisian apartments which make entertaining for lots of people impossible. Plus there's really not much to organizing a picnic – just ask everyone to bring something along and you're sorted. This chapter is full of my personal picnic favourites – I hope you enjoy them.

Quiche Lorraine

Bacon and egg tart

Quiche Lorraine should only be pastry, cream, eggs and bacon. No cheese, no onions, nor any extra flavours. *Quiche* originates from Lorraine, the region of France that borders Germany. The word *quiche* comes from the German word *Kuchen*, meaning cake.

A *quiche* is basically a savoury custard tart. Add bacon and you have *quiche Lorraine*; add some Gruyère cheese and you have *quiche Vosgienne*. Add whatever filling you fancy — see my suggestions below — and you'll have *quiche à la [your name]*!

• 90g soft butter • 1 teaspoon sugar • a pinch of salt
• 180g plain flour • 2 egg yolks • ice-cold water

For the filling • 150g *lardons* or cubes of smoked bacon*
• 4 eggs plus 2 egg yolks (save the whites to brush the pastry)
• 300g *crème fraîche* or double cream • 1 teaspoon salt • pepper

Make the pastry. Using a wooden spoon,** beat together the butter, sugar and salt until soft and creamy. Mix in the flour followed by the egg yolks and 2 tablespoons ice-cold water. Mix and bring together to make a smooth ball, adding a little more water if the pastry is too crumbly (only knead as much as necessary to bring the dough together). Wrap the dough in cling film and refrigerate for a minimum of an hour (best overnight).

Remove the pastry from the fridge 30 minutes before using. Roll out the pastry between 2 sheets of baking paper until it is 5mm thick, and use to line a 25cm quiche tin that is at least 3cm deep. Brush the pastry base with egg white. Refrigerate while preparing the filling.

Preheat the oven to 180°C.

To make the filling, fry the *lardons* in a non-stick frying pan until golden brown, then lift out with a slotted spoon and leave to cool on paper towels. Meanwhile, lightly beat the eggs and egg yolks in a bowl, add the *crème fraîche* and seasoning and continue to beat until mixed together. Scatter the *lardons* in the pastry case and then pour in the egg mix. Bake for 30–45 minutes or until the filling is golden brown and set. Serve warm or cold.

* *Alternative fillings* • *roasted vegetables* • *asparagus and smoked salmon* • *cherry tomatoes, cubes of Cheddar cheese and thyme leaves* • *softened mushrooms and leeks*

** *You can use a food processor to make the pastry, but be careful not to overmix.*

Preparation time: 30 minutes Resting time: 1 hour–overnight
Baking time: 30–45 minutes

Pissaladière

Anchovy, onion and black olive tart

A lot of people think that the Provençal *pissaladière* is the French version of the classic Italian pizza. In fact, *pissaladière* gets its name from *pissala*, a salty fish paste originally used to flavour the dish. Nowadays, the pizza-esque base is topped with anchovies instead of the fish paste, together with slowly cooked onions and black olives.

• 5g dried yeast • 75ml warm water • a pinch of sugar
• 150g strong white flour • ½ teaspoon salt • ½ teaspoon dried rosemary
• 1 tablespoon olive oil, plus extra for brushing

For the topping • 500g large onions, thinly sliced • 8 anchovies,* drained of oil
• 1 tablespoon olive oil, plus extra for drizzling • a pinch of sugar
• finely grated zest of 1 unwaxed orange (optional) • 10 black olives, pitted

Make the base. Dissolve the yeast in the warm water with the sugar. Combine the rest of the dry ingredients in a bowl, pour in the dissolved yeast and the olive oil and mix to form a dough. Turn the dough on to a lightly floured surface and knead until silky smooth and fairly elastic (a good 5 minutes).

Brush a baking tray with olive oil. Roll out the dough until it is 3mm thick (like a thin pizza and any shape you want), then place it on the tray, pushing it a little way up the sides. Brush with olive oil, cover with a damp tea towel and leave to rise in a warm place for 30 minutes.

Meanwhile, make the topping. Gently fry the onions and 2 of the anchovies in 1 tablespoon olive oil for 30–40 minutes. Once the onions are soft and have a marmalade consistency, mix in the sugar and orange zest (if using). Leave to cool for 10 minutes.

Preheat the oven to 200°C. Spread the onions over the dough, followed by the remaining anchovies.** Drizzle some olive oil on top and bake for 20–25 minutes or until the base is golden. Take out of the oven and put the olives on top. Serve warm or cold.

* *The anchovies I buy are the luxury kind that are kept in good olive oil. They are less salty than the tinned fillets you get at the supermarket. If the ones you buy are super salty, they should be rinsed carefully and dried on paper towels.*

** *If you prefer your anchovies juicy rather than crisp, add them with the olives at the end (olives tend to shrivel up and burn if baked).*

Preparation time: 30 minutes Resting time: 30 minutes
Cooking time: about 1 hour

Tarte flambée

Onion and crème fraîche tart

Provence has *Pissaladière*, while in Alsace they have *tarte flambée*, a pizza-style base topped with *crème fraîche, lardons* and onions – popular ingredients in Alsatian cuisine.

Gluten-free is a concept that hasn't quite caught on in the land of *baguettes*, and it can be frustrating for anyone on a gluten-free diet who wants to try delicious French pastries and bread, so here I've replaced the regular wheat base with chestnut flour and tapioca starch. This means no kneading is required – just mix the ingredients together to form a ball.

• 160g chestnut flour* • 140g tapioca starch • 1 teaspoon guar gum**
• 1½ teaspoons baking powder • ½ teaspoon salt • 1 tablespoon light soft brown sugar
• 5g dried yeast • ½ teaspoon sugar • 190ml warm water

For the topping • 4 tablespoons *crème fraîche* • 2 red onions, thinly sliced
• 100g *lardons* or cubes of smoked bacon • 4 sprigs of thyme, leaves only

Mix together the flour, tapioca starch, guar gum, baking powder, salt and sugar in a large bowl. Make a well in the middle. Dissolve the dried yeast and sugar in the warm water. When the yeast begins to foam, pour it into the well and mix everything together to form a ball. Roll out the dough between 2 pieces of baking paper until 5mm thick, then place in a baking tin that is large enough for the pastry to sit flat. (The shape doesn't really matter, it's the 5mm thickness that's important.) Remove the top layer of paper and trim off any excess paper from around the bottom edges.

Preheat the oven to 200°C and place a large baking tray in the oven to get hot.

Spread the *crème fraîche* over the dough, then sprinkle the onions, *lardons* and thyme leaves on top. Slide the baking tin on to the hot baking tray and bake for 20–30 minutes or until the edges are crisp. The tart is traditionally eaten warm, but it's great cold too.

* *Chestnut flour can be bought in health food shops and online. For tapioca starch, try your supermarket or a Chinese grocery store.*

** *Guar gum is a very powerful thickening agent made from guar beans. You can find it in powdered form online and in health food shops.*

Alternative idea

• *For a sweet topping, replace the onions and lardons with thinly sliced apples and a sprinkle of ground cinnamon and brown sugar.*

Preparation time: 30 minutes   Baking time: 20–30 minutes

Cake au saucisson sec avec pistaches et prunes

Cured sausage, pistachio and prune cake

A cake with cured sausage, pistachio and prunes? *Pourquoi pas?* The French have been making savoury cakes for quite a while. They appear in *boulangeries* and with a side salad on lunch menus in chic cafés, and they're most likely to appear at a picnic (my first encounter). They are super-simple to make and can be adapted to use whatever leftovers you have in your fridge – roasted vegetables, cold meats, cheese. Just follow the basic batter recipe and get creative with the fillings.

• 250g plain flour • 15g baking powder • 150g cured French sausage or salami, finely chopped • 80g pistachios, roughly chopped • 100g prunes, roughly chopped • 4 eggs • 100ml milk • 150ml olive oil • 50g plain yoghurt • 1 teaspoon salt • pepper

Preheat the oven to 180°C and line a 500g loaf tin with baking paper. In a bowl, mix together the flour, baking powder, sausage, pistachios and prunes. In a separate bowl, whisk the eggs until thick and pale in colour. Gradually whisk in the milk, oil and yoghurt, then add the salt and pepper and fold in the flour mixture bit by bit. Try not to overbeat (it's better to undermix).*

Pour the batter into the prepared tin. Bake for 30–40 minutes or until a metal skewer inserted in the centre of the cake comes out clean. Leave to cool in the tin.

* Pourquoi?

The more the batter is beaten when the flour is added, the more the gluten gets developed. For cakes and pastries too much gluten is not desirable (unlike for bread) as it makes the end result tough. To prevent overbeating when adding the flour, you may find it easier to use a rubber spatula rather than a whisk.

Preparation time: 20 minutes Baking time: 30–40 minutes

Salade de carrottes râpées et rémoulade de céleri-rave et pommes

Carrot salad and Celeriac and apple salad

Carrot and celeriac salads are staples on many lunch menus. There's not much to the recipes, just the main ingredient and a *vinaigrette*, and therein lies the pleasure. So simple that they can be effortlessly whipped up for a picnic in a matter of minutes.

For the carrot salad • **8 carrots, grated*** • **½ bunch of parsley, finely chopped**
• **5 tablespoons sunflower oil** • **juice of ½ lemon** • **salt and pepper**

For the celeriac and apple salad • **250g celeriac, grated*** • **1 dessert apple, peeled and grated***
• **5 tablespoons sunflower oil** • **2 tablespoons white wine vinegar**
• **1 heaped teaspoon grainy mustard** • **a pinch of sugar** • **salt and pepper**

To make the carrot salad, put the carrots and parsley into a bowl. Make a *vinaigrette* by mixing together the oil and lemon juice with salt and pepper to taste. Pour the *vinaigrette* over the carrots and toss everything together. Taste for seasoning.**

To make the celeriac and apple salad, put the celeriac and apple into a bowl. Make a *vinaigrette* by mixing together the oil, wine vinegar, mustard, sugar and salt and pepper to taste. Pour the *vinaigrette* over the celeriac and apple and toss everything together. Taste for seasoning.**

* *If you have a grating attachment on your food processor to make fine little matchsticks, use this rather than a traditional grater. A bit more work, but the texture of the matchsticks creates a crunchier salad.*

** *Both salads are best eaten on the day you make them (celeriac and apple has a tendency to discolour, even with the dressing). Keep them in separate airtight containers in the fridge until it's time to take them to the picnic.*

Preparation time: 20 minutes (for both salads)

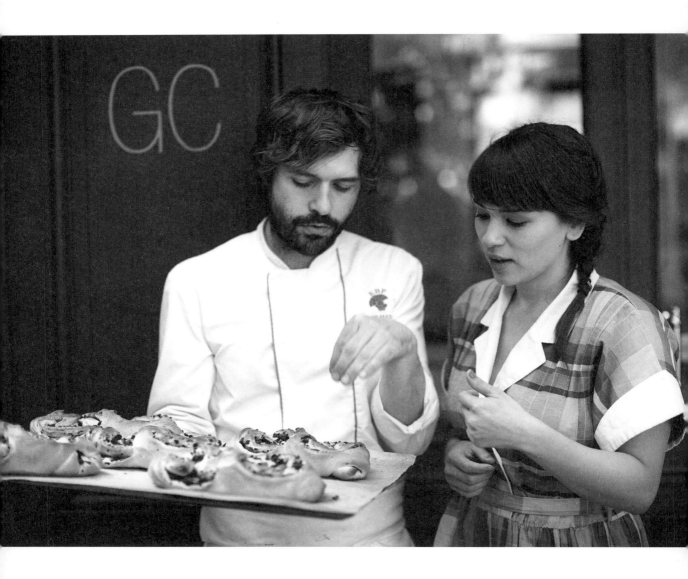

'Choosing bread in a boulangerie can be quite overwhelming. Of course, there's the classic baguette but there's also a whole range of other breads such as sourdough, wholegrain and rye, and breads with nuts, figs and other dried fruit'

Pain brié

Olive bread

This recipe was given to me by Gontran Cherrier, who comes from a family of bakers going back three generations. He has several cookbooks under his belt and runs a Parisian bakery, so when it comes to bread he certainly knows what he's talking about. His *pain brié* is typical of the Normandy region and is simple to make. I baked it for a picnic and it must have been good – by the time I wanted to try some, it was all gone.

• 5g dried yeast • 4 tablespoons warm water • 85g plain flour • a generous pinch of salt
• a knob of soft butter • 300g fermented dough*

For the filling • 50g green olives, pitted • 50g black olives, pitted
• 1 teaspoon finely chopped rosemary (optional) • 20ml olive oil

Dissolve the yeast in the warm water. Mix the flour and salt together in a large bowl. Add the dissolved yeast, butter and fermented dough, and bring together to form a ball. Turn the ball out on to a floured surface and knead for 15 minutes or until the dough becomes smooth. Cover with a damp tea towel and leave to rise in a warm place for 30 minutes.

To make the filling, mix together the olives and rosemary (if using) with the olive oil.

Roll out the dough on a floured surface to a rectangle that is about 1cm thick and slightly larger than a sheet of A4 paper. Spread the olive mixture on top. Roll up the dough lengthways to form a large sausage, then place join-side down on a piece of baking paper. Using a sharp knife, cut deep slits in the dough to reveal the layers of olives (but don't cut all the way down to the bottom). Cover again with a damp tea towel and leave to rise in a warm place for an hour or until doubled in size.

Preheat the oven to 240°C** with a baking tray in the middle and a roasting tin at the bottom. Once the oven is hot, slide the bread on to the hot baking tray (keeping it on the paper) and pour a glass of water into the roasting tin. Bake the loaf for 5 minutes, then reduce the temperature to 210°C and bake for a further 20–25 minutes. Transfer to a wire rack and serve warm or cold.

*** For the fermented dough,** ask your baker, or make it yourself the night before. Mix 10g dried yeast with 130ml warm water. Stir until dissolved. Mix 200g plain flour with 2 generous pinches of salt. Pour in the dissolved yeast and mix together. Knead until it forms a smooth ball (it will be sticky at the beginning), place in a bowl and cover with cling film. Leave in a warm place for 1 hour, then refrigerate overnight.*

*** Fan-assisted ovens can dry out the bread, so use the regular (non-fan) setting for this loaf if you can.*

Preparation time: 30 minutes   Resting time: several hours, plus overnight   Baking time: 25–30 minutes

Clafoutis – versions sucré et salé

Sweet and savoury clafoutis

Clafoutis originally came from the Limousin. Baked fruit in a simple batter of eggs, sugar, ground almonds and flour, it's the kind of dessert your French *grand-mère* would make if you had one. Traditionally whole cherries are used, but you can use whatever fruit you have. You can even get away with tinned fruit, as long as you drain it well.

The French have recently taken to transforming dessert recipes into savoury ones. Replace the fruit with cheese and tomatoes, leave out the sugar and *voilà* – a savoury *clafoutis*.

• 4 eggs • 150g sugar • a pinch of salt • 50g ground almonds*
• 2 tablespoons plain flour • 100g *crème fraîche* • 100ml milk
• 350g cherries, pitted, or any soft fruit or berries of your choice (or even chocolate chunks)

Preheat the oven to 180°C and butter and flour a 19 × 10cm baking dish or tin.** Whisk the eggs with the sugar and salt until pale yellow and thick. Sift and fold in the ground almonds and flour, then stir in the *crème fraîche* and milk. Scatter the cherries in the prepared dish, spreading them out evenly. Pour the batter over the cherries and bake for 30–40 minutes or until golden brown and set. Serve warm or cold.

Savoury clafoutis

Make as for the sweet clafoutis but omit the sugar, replacing the cherries with 100g mature cheese (e.g. Gruyère, mature Comté, Cheddar or goat's cheese), chopped into large cubes, 100g cherry tomatoes and 50g black olives, pitted. You could also flavour the batter with chopped herbs, such as basil, parsley or thyme, and use leftover roasted vegetables as an alternative to the cheese and tomatoes.

* *Almonds can be replaced with different ground nuts, such as hazelnuts or pistachios.*

** *Or make individual clafoutis: butter and flour 6–8 ramekins (roughly 8cm in diameter and 4cm deep). Divide the cherries and batter between the ramekins and bake for 15–20 minutes. You can turn them out for serving if you like.*

Preparation time: 15 minutes   Baking time: 30–40 minutes

Fougasse aux romarin, lavande et fromage du chèvre

Rosemary, lavender and goat's cheese bread

The word *fougasse* stems from the ancient Roman *panis focacius*, which is probably why the bread is so similar to the Italian *focaccia*. Unlike the Italians, however, the French stretch and slice their loaf into a leaf shape. This isn't just for aesthetic reasons — the slashes increase the surface area of the bread, ensuring a crisper, faster-cooking loaf.

The bread makes a great base for any topping you fancy: leftover roasted vegetables, cheese, fruit, herbs — the possibilities are endless.

- 10g dried yeast • 250ml lukewarm water • 400g strong white flour
- 1½ teaspoons salt, plus extra for sprinkling • 1 teaspoon dried rosemary
- ½ teaspoon dried lavender • 2 tablespoons olive oil, plus extra for brushing
- 80g hard goat's cheese, cut into small cubes

Mix the yeast with the warm water, stirring until the yeast has completely dissolved. Mix the flour, salt, rosemary and lavender in a bowl. Pour in the dissolved yeast and the olive oil and mix to form a dough. Turn the dough on to a lightly floured surface and knead until it forms a smooth, sticky ball (don't add too much flour as it's better sticky). Cover with cling film and leave to rise in a warm place for an hour, then put in the fridge overnight.

The following day, turn the dough on to a floured surface and knead for 5 minutes or until it forms a smooth ball again, then cover with a damp tea towel and leave to rise in a warm place for 30 minutes.

Roll out the dough to a large rectangle and then cut the rectangle diagonally into 2 triangles. Make a large cut down the middle of each triangle without cutting all the way through the dough, starting a little way in from the short edge and stopping before the opposite corner. Make 3 small slashes on each side of the cut, then use your fingers to gently open out the slashes to look like the veins of a leaf. Place each triangle on a piece of baking paper and push the cubes of cheese randomly into the dough. Cover with a damp tea towel and leave to rise in a warm place for an hour or until doubled in size.

Preheat the oven to 240°C and put a baking tray in the oven to get hot. Brush the bread with olive oil and sprinkle with a couple of pinches of salt. Once the oven is hot, place the bread on the hot baking tray and bake for 5 minutes, then reduce the temperature to 210°C and bake for a further 12–15 minutes or until the bread is golden brown. Best eaten warm.

Preparation time: 30 minutes Resting time: overnight, plus 2 hours
Baking time: 17–20 minutes

Crème Vichyssoise au chou-fleur glacé

Iced cauliflower and potato soup

Depending who you believe, Vichyssoise is either a French or an American invention. Nobody can really say for sure. One story claims that the French chef Louis Diat created it in 1914 for the Ritz–Carlton Hotel in New York City. He grew up not far from the French spa town of Vichy, which is why he named the soup Vichyssoise.

The traditional recipe calls for leeks and potatoes, but I have swapped the leeks for cauliflower, which makes a milder-tasting soup. Make it the day before serving so that it has enough time to chill, then all you need do before the picnic is pop it into a flask.

- 1 small head of cauliflower (600g), chopped into florets – you can use some of the stalks
- 240g potatoes, cut into large chunks • 1 onion, chopped • a knob of butter
- 1.2 litres hot chicken or vegetable stock • 600ml milk
- 100g *crème fraîche*, plus a little extra for serving • salt and white pepper
- a handful of chopped chives

Gently fry the vegetables in the butter for 5 minutes or until the onion is soft but not golden. Add the hot stock and simmer for 20 minutes or until the potatoes and cauliflower are soft. Leave to cool slightly before stirring in the milk and *crème fraîche*, then whizz in an electric blender until smooth and season with salt and pepper.

Refrigerate the soup until cold for at least 4 hours, preferably overnight. Taste for seasoning before serving extra cold, garnished with a dollop of *crème fraîche* and some chopped chives.

Preparation time: 30 minutes Cooking time: 25 minutes
Chilling time: 4 hours–overnight

Cervelles de canut

Fresh cheese with shallots and red wine

Literally translated, *cervelles de canut* means silk worker's brains. Fear not – no cannibalism, nor even carnivorism, is committed here. The recipe originated in Lyon, which was made the capital of French silk production by Louis XI in 1466. It is thought that by the nineteenth century the silk workers were treated with such disdain by high society in the city that they named this simple dish after them.

• 250g *fromage frais* (to make your own, see page 96) or cottage cheese
• 50g *crème fraîche* • 1 tablespoon red wine vinegar • 1 small shallot, finely chopped
• ½ clove of garlic, crushed to a paste • ½ teaspoon sugar
• 4 tablespoons finely chopped chives • salt and pepper

Drain any excess liquid from the cheese. Mix all the ingredients together in a bowl, saving some of the chives for the garnish, and taste for seasoning. Cover the bowl and refrigerate the cheese for 2 hours.*

Sprinkle the cheese with chives and serve chilled, with fresh bread and raw vegetables like carrot sticks, peppers and radishes.

* Can be kept in an airtight container in the fridge for several days.

Preparation time: 10 minutes   Chilling time: 2 hours

LE THON

LE COCKTAIL

LES PISTACHES

LA MENTHE

LE CÈPE

LE RADIS

LES OIGNONS FRAIS

L'HUITRE

LES CHANTERELLES

LA SALADE

L'AIL

LE PASTIS

LES OLIVES

LES CORNICHONS

UNE COUPE DE CHAMPAGNE

Aperitifs

Apéros

LE COCKTAIL

LE CÈPE

LES PISTACHES

LE CONCOMBRE

LA SALADE

LE PASTIS

LES OLIVES

LE THON

LES CORNICHONS

LES OIGNONS FRAIS

L'HUITRE

LA RÂPE

L'AIL

LA MENTHE

'*La bonne cuisine est la base du véritable bonheur*' ('Good food is the foundation of true happiness') is what the famous French chef Auguste Escoffier said, and I couldn't agree more. And what more pleasurable way to kick off an evening than with a glass of something red, white or bubbly and a delicious nibble or two? *L'heure de l'apéro* could be considered the French version of the cocktail hour, except that there are no chips and dips on the menu, but instead you might find a selection of charcuterie (cured meats) served with some crunchy *cornichons* (little gherkins).

Like many traditions in France, *l'heure de l'apéro* is considered a perfect opportunity to indulge oneself, to take a moment after a hard day at work to unwind. The practice came from the nineteeth-century French custom of a '*coup d'avant*' ('shot before'). This was usually a shot of Vermouth, and only served to men. Vermouth (an essential ingredient for a dry Martini) was created in 1813 by herbalist Joseph Noilly, who claimed Vermouth had health benefits (most aperitifs of the time made this claim). The manufacturing process has hardly changed. Grapes from Marseillan are matured in oak casks and subsequently blended with a secret mix of spices and herbs.

Another old-school favourite is *pastis*, an aniseed-flavoured liqueur which is mixed with water.

Although Paris in the last couple of years has seen the rise of cocktails, the French still prefer to keep it simple. The closest the French get to a cocktail would be a Kir (a splash of *crème de cassis* with white wine) or Kir royal (*crème de cassis* with champagne).

No matter what drinks and nibbles you decide to serve, I think the most important part is taking the time to slow down and relax. And that is most certainly a health benefit in today's crazy, hectic world.

SERVES 4

Pâté de foie de lapin

Rabbit liver pâté

It's funny how some things you couldn't stand eating as a kid you start to love when you're a grown-up. Liver used to be like that for me. My mum would try to find creative ways of disguising it, but I could smell liver a mile off. This all changed when I took an intensive two-week cookery course and discovered that livers can be delicious, especially when made into a pâté. The trick is not to overcook them.

• 100g salted butter • 1 shallot, thinly sliced • 2 cloves of garlic, pounded flat
• 2 bay leaves • 2 sprigs of thyme • 225g rabbit livers,* trimmed and cleaned
• 1 tablespoon Cognac • 1 small anchovy fillet • ½ teaspoon pepper • salt (if necessary)

For the clarified butter • 160g unsalted butter

Melt a knob of the salted butter in a large pan and add the shallot, garlic, bay leaves and thyme. Cook until the shallot is softened but not brown. Add the livers and Cognac and cook for about 2 minutes on each side or until the livers are browned on the outside but still pink in the middle. Leave to cool for 5 minutes. Remove the bay leaves and thyme and then whizz the livers in an electric blender with the anchovy and the rest of the salted butter. Add the pepper and check for seasoning. Divide the pâté between 4 ramekins (about 6cm in diameter and 4cm deep)** and smooth the tops.

To make the clarified butter, melt the unsalted butter in a saucepan and bring to a boil. Be careful, as it may splatter. Take off the heat and leave to stand for a few minutes, then remove the crusty white layer from the top. Underneath the crust will be the clear (clarified) butter. Pour this clear butter over the pâté in the ramekins, and discard the milky liquid at the bottom. Wrap the ramekins in cling film and refrigerate for a minimum of 4 hours (or overnight) before serving. The pâté will keep refrigerated for up to a week or frozen for up to 2 months.

The livers from farmed rabbits are mild in flavour, like chicken livers (which you can also use for this recipe). Wild rabbit livers are strong-tasting and will need soaking in milk overnight before use, so that they lose some of their 'gamey' flavour.

** Or make 1 large pâté in a 500g loaf tin.*

Preparation time: 20 minutes Cooking time: 15 minutes
Chilling time: 4 hours–overnight

Terrine forestière

Wild mushroom terrine

When I was a child, I used to go mushroom-hunting with my parents. This was long before foraging became fashionable with Michelin-starred restaurants. Looking for *chanterelles*, *cèpes*, *trompettes de la mort* and many other forest fungi was a bit of a bore for my brother and me, and we would always hope for a rainy day (although a light drizzle wouldn't put my parents off). Needless to say, I don't do much foraging now that I live in Paris, although I like to think that going to the Parisian flea markets could be classed as urban foraging.

• 450g mixed wild mushrooms • 2 knobs of butter • 2 shallots, finely chopped
• 2 cloves of garlic, crushed to a paste • 4 eggs • 250g *crème fraîche*
• 2 teaspoons Dijon mustard • a pinch of nutmeg
• 2 tablespoons chopped parsley • salt and pepper

Preheat the oven to 160°C and line two 250g mini loaf tins* with baking paper.

Clean the mushrooms carefully with paper towels or a brush, then roughly chop any that are large to make them all about the same size. Melt the butter in a large frying pan and add the shallots and garlic. Once the shallots begin to brown, add the mushrooms and fry for a good 10 minutes until they have released all their juices (if the pan is too small for them all in one go, fry in batches).

Meanwhile, beat the eggs in a bowl with the *crème fraîche* and mustard. Add the nutmeg and parsley and season with salt and pepper.

Remove the cooked mushroom mixture from the pan with a slotted spoon (to drain off any liquid) and divide between the prepared tins. Pour the *crème fraîche* mix over the mushrooms and bake for about 15 minutes or until set. Leave to cool slightly before cutting. Best served at room temperature.

Or make 1 large terrine in a 500g loaf tin and bake for about 30 minutes or until set.

Preparation time: 20 minutes Cooking time: 15 minutes

Rillettes au porc

Coarse pork pâté

Rillettes are almost always found sitting on a platter of *charcuterie*, but you won't find many people making them at home. They're the kind of thing usually bought ready-made from the supermarket or butcher. The best ones are made from fatty meats, like belly pork, goose or duck, which are slowly roasted to allow the fat to melt. Everything is then blended to make a coarse pâté, a little seasoning is added, and that's it.

• 1kg boned pork belly with skin* • 2 bay leaves
• 1 sprig of rosemary • 2 sprigs of thyme • salt and pepper

Preheat the oven to 130°C. Chop the pork into large pieces and place in a large baking tray with the bay leaves, rosemary and thyme. Cover the tray with aluminium foil and cook for 3 hours, stirring halfway.

Remove the tray from the oven and leave the pork to cool.

Peel the skin** off the pork. Discard the bay, rosemary and thyme, and put the meat into an electric blender with any fat from the tray. Whizz to a rough paste and season to taste with salt and pepper. Transfer to a serving dish and serve at room temperature.

The *rillettes* will keep in an airtight container in the fridge for 3–4 days (the fat will harden when chilled, and the *rillettes* will need to be broken up with a fork before serving).

You can replace the pork belly with boned duck legs.

** *I put the skin under a very hot grill for a couple of minutes to make crackling, then I cut it into small bits and season with salt before serving.*

Preparation time: 30 minutes Cooking time: 3 hours

Rillettes de canard
Poids net : 180g

Paté Campagne
ou piment d'Espelette
Poids net : 180g

TERRÍNES "MAIS
RILLETTES CANARD
FOIE CANARD FOIE GRAS
BOUDÍN "PORC NOIR BIGORR
CAMPAGNE "PIMENT ESPELE
JAMBONNEAU   P⁷E
"PORC NOIR BIGORRE G

Rouleaux de salade Niçoise

Salad Niçoise wraps

Trying to find out what an authentic Salade Niçoise should be made of is like solving a cryptic puzzle. Tuna or no tuna? Cooked vegetables or not? After an extensive survey amongst my foodie and French friends, I came to the conclusion that as long as it contains ingredients you would find in the vicinity of the Provençal town of Nice, then you can more or less call it a Salade Niçoise.

- a pinch each of salt and sugar • 12 green beans, topped and tailed • 1 Little Gem lettuce
- 1 red *endive* (chicory) • 12 anchovies,* drained and boned
- 12 black olives (preferably from Nice), pitted and sliced
- 6 cherry tomatoes, quartered or halved depending on size • 6 radishes, thinly sliced
- 1 spring onion, thinly sliced • 2 soft-boiled eggs, peeled and each cut into 6 wedges
- 2 tablespoons capers, finely chopped

For the vinaigrette • 2 tablespoons red wine vinegar • 4 tablespoons extra virgin olive oil
• ¼ clove of garlic, crushed to a paste • juice of ½ lemon • a pinch of sugar • salt and pepper

Make the *vinaigrette* by whisking all the ingredients together in a bowl. Taste for seasoning.

Bring a large pot of water to a boil. Add the salt and sugar followed by the green beans. Blanch for 2 minutes, then drain and rinse under cold running water.

Separate the lettuce and endive into individual leaves – you will need 12 leaves in total. Divide the remaining ingredients between the leaves, halving the beans if they are long (they should be slightly shorter than the length of the leaves). Drizzle some *vinaigrette* on top and serve the rest in a small bowl.

* *I prefer using the plump Provençal anchovies that are preserved in olive oil. These tend to be less salty than tinned anchovy fillets, which need to be carefully rinsed and dried on paper towels before use.*

Additional ingredients

- *boiled small potatoes, halved or quartered*
- *sweetcorn*
- *tuna – season a 200g piece of raw tuna (preferably yellowfin) and sear in a smoking hot pan with a little olive oil for a minute on each side, then cut into thin slices.*

Preparation time: 20 minutes Cooking time: 5 minutes

'No matter what you decide to serve, I think the most important part is taking the time to slow down and relax. And that is most certainly a health benefit in today's crazy, hectic world'

Palmiers et sacristains sâlés

Elephant ears and puff pastry twists

I remember having to make puff pastry at cookery school during a really hot summer. Our air conditioning was broken and the kitchen was hot from the previous class, so my pastry and I were both melting in the heat. Not ideal! The pastry had to go into the fridge numerous times before I could finish making it, and I wished I could have got into the fridge myself.

Not wanting to waste any of the puff pastry after spending so much time and effort making it, we used the leftovers to make sweet *palmiers* and *sacristains* with sugar and cinnamon.

Nowadays I save myself the hassle and order puff pastry from my local *boulangerie*. Otherwise, you can buy pretty good puff pastry from the supermarket – make sure you get the all-butter version.

• 250g puff pastry

For the palmiers • 1 heaped tablespoon Meaux mustard (or another grainy mustard)
• 2 handfuls of finely grated mature Comté cheese or a mature hard cheese of your choice

For the sacristains • 20 olives, pitted • 1 clove of garlic • 1 anchovy fillet

Preheat the oven to 200°C and line 2 baking trays with baking paper. Roll out the dough between 2 sheets of baking paper into a 40 × 30cm rectangle. Cut the rectangle in half widthways, to give two 20 × 30cm rectangles.

To make the *palmiers*, spread the mustard over 1 pastry rectangle and sprinkle the cheese on top. Take 1 long side of the rectangle and roll it into the middle. Repeat on the other side, so that the 2 rolls touch each other. Wrap tightly in cling film and freeze for 10 minutes* before cutting into thirty 1cm slices. Lay the slices on one of the prepared baking trays.

To make the *sacristains*, crush the olives, garlic and anchovy to a rough paste *(tapenade)* using a mortar and pestle or an electric blender. Spread the *tapenade* over the remaining pastry rectangle and then cut the rectangle into twelve 2.5cm-wide strips. Take a strip and twist it, then lay it on the second baking tray. Repeat with the remaining strips.

Bake the *palmiers* and *sacristains* for 10 minutes or until golden and crisp. Serve warm or at room temperature.

* *Both* palmiers *and* sacristains *can be frozen unbaked. Simply bake from frozen, allowing an extra couple of minutes in the oven.*

Preparation time: 30 minutes Resting time: 10 minutes
Baking time: 10 minutes

Truffes de foie gras

Foie gras truffles

One of my favourite restaurants in Paris is Le Châteaubriand, despite the fact you're at the whims of the chef, Inaki Aizpitarte, when you eat there (it's a set menu only). I've always been impressed with the way Aizpitarte combines his love of foreign cuisines with his French origins, but what I enjoy most is that the dishes are simple yet always with a special touch that makes them original.

One of the starters I have enjoyed there is *foie gras* sprinkled with Indian *mukhwas*, an after-dinner nibble of spice seeds and nuts that tastes sweet and refreshing. I was surprised how well they went together, and also that I actually ate it – *foie gras* is one of the very few foods I prefer not to eat. The whole thing got me thinking about sweet and savoury combinations, and that's how this little idea came about.

- 200g *foie gras, Faux Gras** or duck liver pâté • 2 tablespoons unsweetened cocoa powder
- 2 tablespoons crushed ginger biscuits • 2 tablespoons *mukhwas*

Place the *foie gras* in the freezer and freeze for 10 minutes until well chilled.

Cut the *foie gras* into 15–20 x 1.5cm cubes and roll into balls.** Roll some of the balls in cocoa powder, some in crushed biscuits and others in *mukhwas*. Chill for at least 30 minutes or until needed. Serve in *petit four* or sweetie cases, with small triangles of toast.

* Faux Gras *is made from the livers of geese and ducks that have been naturally fattened rather than force-fed.*

** *If the pâté starts melting in your hands, place it back in the freezer and run your hands under cold water.*

**Preparation time: 20 minutes Resting time: 10 minutes
Chilling time: 30 minutes**

Les huîtres

Oysters

When to eat oysters? Well, oysters spawn in the warmer months (May to August), which makes them fatty, watery and lacking in flavour at this time of year, whereas oysters that are harvested in the cooler, non-spawning months (the ones with the letter 'r' in them) have a fresh seafood flavour and are lean with a firm texture. It's as simple as that.

Buying and storing oysters

Oysters should be tightly closed and unbroken when bought. Discard any that open. They can be kept unopened, wrapped in wet paper towels, for a couple of days in the fridge. Don't store them in an airtight container or in fresh water as they will die.

How to shuck an oyster

Use a special oyster knife (called a shucker) that has a guard and a dull blade with a pointed tip. Don't even attempt to use an ordinary knife, as you'll be more likely to stab yourself than open the oyster.

Wash and scrub the oysters under cold running water to get them clean. Using a tea towel folded double to protect your hand, place the oyster with its round bottom on a chopping board. Dig the tip of the knife into the hinge (the pointy end of the oyster) and wiggle the blade along the hinge in order to loosen it. Once the shell is loose enough, twist the knife to open the shell a little. Imagine turning a key in a car door.

Keep the knife flush with the top shell and slide it along to separate the two shells and sever the muscle in the top shell.

Lift off the top shell and remove any broken pieces of shell from the oyster flesh, being careful not to spill any of the juices.

Should the oyster smell in any way fishy or 'off', discard it. Freshly shucked oysters should smell of the sea in a clean, fresh and pleasant way.

If you want to make the oyster easier to eat, carefully detach the muscle from the bottom shell with the tip of the knife.

Les assaisonnements pour les huîtres – Condiments for oysters

An oyster purist would frown upon eating anything but the oyster, but for me a squeeze of lemon or the traditional *mignonette* takes the edge off the feeling of gulping down a mouthful of seawater. I also have my favourite condiments to serve with them, but go easy – you don't want to drown out the oyster's flavour.

In general when I serve oysters I reckon with at least 8 per person (the French absolutely love oysters). Each condiment recipe on page 145 is enough for 12–15 oysters (you only need about ½ teaspoon of condiment with each one as it shouldn't mask the flavour of the oyster itself). All condiments should be refrigerated for an hour before using.

Mignonette

• a pinch of sugar • a pinch of salt • 2 tablespoons red wine vinegar • 1 shallot, finely diced

Dissolve the sugar and salt in the vinegar, then mix in the chopped shallot.

Calvados apple mignonette

• a pinch of sugar • a pinch of salt • 1 tablespoon cider vinegar
• 1 teaspoon Calvados • ¼ Granny Smith apple, cored and finely diced

Dissolve the sugar and salt in the vinegar and Calvados, then mix in the apple.

Watermelon and cucumber brunoise*

• a pinch of salt • a generous pinch of sugar • 2 tablespoons rice wine vinegar
• 4 tablespoons finely diced watermelon flesh (without skin and seeds)
• 3 tablespoons finely diced deseeded cucumber

Dissolve the salt and sugar in the vinegar and pour over the watermelon and cucumber. Mix carefully together.

* Brunoise *is the French term for ingredients that have been finely diced into tiny cubes.*

Le grand aïoli avec des crudités

Garlic mayonnaise with crunchy raw vegetables

Le grand aïoli is traditionally a main course, but instead of serving the garlic mayonnaise the classic way with boiled vegetables, I serve it with raw vegetables (or *crudités* as the French call them), for extra freshness and crunch.

• a selection of seasonal raw vegetables (e.g. carrots, radishes, peppers, *endive*/chicory leaves and cherry tomatoes), enough for 4 people

For the aïoli • 1 slice of white bread, crusts removed • 4 tablespoons milk
• 4 cloves of garlic • 1 egg yolk • 250ml olive oil (not extra virgin)
• 3 tablespoons lemon juice • salt and pepper

Prepare the vegetables for dipping, leaving the stalks on for an attractive presentation.

To make the *aïoli*, soak the bread in the milk for 10 minutes.

Squeeze out any excess liquid from the bread, then pound the bread and garlic to a smooth paste using a mortar and pestle. Add the egg yolk and continue pounding, then start adding the olive oil a few drops at a time. Keep on pounding, slowly incorporating the remaining oil until the mayonnaise is thick, then add the lemon juice and salt and pepper to taste. If not using immediately, keep in an airtight container in the fridge and use within a day. Whisk before serving, as it sometimes sets a little stiff when chilled.

Serve the *aïoli* in a bowl, surrounded by the vegetables for dipping.

Preparation time: 20 minutes

Financiers en apéritif

Aperitif financiers

According to legend, these little cakes were made by a *pâtissier* who baked in La Bourse, the financial district of Paris. He made little cakes in the shape of gold bars to sell to his financial clients, hence the name *financiers*.

Traditionally, *financiers* are sweet, but they can easily be made into a savoury bite for an *apéro*, and the filling can be any ingredients you have in your fridge. Just make sure you cut them into small pieces.

• 100g butter • 75g ground almonds • 30g plain flour • 1½ teaspoons baking powder
• ½ teaspoon sugar • 3 eggs, separated • ½ teaspoon salt

For the filling • 150g cheese, ham, bacon, olives, cherry tomatoes or
leftover roasted vegetables (whatever you fancy really)

Preheat the oven to 180°C and butter and flour a financier tin.*

Start melting the butter in a pan over a medium heat. Carry on melting until the butter turns a dark golden brown (this is called *beurre noisette*), then immediately take the pan off the heat.

Mix the dry ingredients together in a bowl. Whisk the egg whites and salt to soft peaks in another bowl.

Beat the egg yolks in a third bowl, and slowly incorporate the warm butter (if the butter is still very hot, it will curdle the eggs). Sift the dry ingredients into the egg and butter mix and then fold in half the egg whites followed by the filling ingredients. Fold in the rest of the egg whites.

Spoon the batter into the prepared tin and bake for 12–15 minutes or until the cakes spring back when touched. Leave to cool in the tin. *Financiers* are best eaten the same day, but will keep in an airtight container for a couple of days.

* Financier *tins usually have 20 sections, so for this recipe you will have to use the tin twice to make 30* financiers. *I have two types of tin at home – an old-fashioned metal one that needs to be buttered and floured, and a new silicone one that needs no preparation. You could use a mini tart tin instead, but you won't get the characteristic gold bar shape that gives* financiers *their name.*

Preparation time: 20 minutes Baking time: 12–15 minutes

Bâtonnets de pastis

Pastis popsicles

Pastis, the anise-flavoured alcohol that is normally diluted with water (it's pretty necessary with a 40 per cent alcohol content), has a bit of a reputation as a drink for pensioners who play *pétanque*. For my generation I thought I'd give *pastis* a little twist and a few extra ingredients. Think *mojito* meets the South of France. Frozen into ice lollies, I think it's quite a refreshing way to start an *apéro*.

• a handful of mint, leaves only • 1 unwaxed lemon
• 1 teaspoon sugar • 160ml lemonade • 40ml *pastis*

Place a mint leaf in each of 12 mini demi-sphere moulds.* Finely grate the lemon zest into a jug. Add the rest of the mint and the sugar to the lemon zest and mash with the end of a rolling pin or a wooden spoon. Mix in 20ml lemon juice, the lemonade and *pastis*. Pass through a sieve and pour into a jug.

Pour the liquid into the moulds and freeze them for 3 hours or until solid. Remove 2 demi spheres and place them back into one of the empty demi-sphere holes to form a sphere (you need to sit the demi spheres upright). Insert an ice-lolly stick into the gap between the 2 demi spheres and pour in a teaspoon of cold water to help them stick together. Repeat with the other spheres to make another 5 popsicles, working quickly. Refreeze for another hour or overnight, until completely frozen.

* *I use a silicone mould that has 15 demi-sphere holes, but if you haven't got a mould you can use an ordinary ice-cube tray to make 6–8 popsicles (depending on the size of your tray). Pour the liquid into the compartments in the tray, then place in the freezer and leave for a couple of hours until semi-frozen. Remove from the freezer and insert an ice-lolly stick into the middle of each popsicle, then return to the freezer until completely frozen.*

Preparation time: 20 minutes Freezing time: 4 hours–overnight

UNE PLANCHE À DÉCOUPER

LES ALLUMETTES

LE MOULIN À POIVRE

LA POÊLE

UNE CUILLÈRE À BOIS

LE BEURRE

UN VERRE DE VIN

LE COUTEAU

LA COCOTTE

LE RÉCHAUD À GAZ

Dinner with Friends and Family

Dîner avec les amis
et la famille

LE MOULIN À POIVRE

LE TABLIER

UNE CUILLÈRE À BOIS

LES ALLUMETTES

LE SEL

LE BOL

L'HEURE DU DÉJEUNER

LA POÊLE

LE BEURRE

L'HUILE D'OLIVE

UNE PLANCHE À DÉCOUPER

In 2010 UNESCO added French gastronomy and the ritual of the traditional French meal to its 'world's intangible heritage' list.

When I first moved to France, I didn't understand what the big fuss was about. After all, there are many other cultures that have culinary traditions that match the French. But I came to realize that it's not just about the cooking, it's about the appreciation of good food. The French understand their produce and know how it should be treated. A great example is the iconic yet humble baguette. In Paris an annual prize is awarded to the best baguette in the region. Even something as basic and affordable as bread is not taken for granted, and it's seen as not only a skill but a form of art.

The French are brought up with this understanding. It doesn't need to be taught. It's a way of life. As UNESCO acknowledged, a French meal is not only about eating. The custom of bringing people together to enjoy good food, drink and company is something the French do particularly well. It starts off with an *apéritif*, followed by four courses (starter, main course, cheese and dessert) and is finished off with a *digestif*. Dishes are carefully matched with wine. French seasonal produce, preferably local, is preferred over foreign, imported products. This is not something new. Long before 'foodtainment', celebrity chefs and the mass food media influx, i.e. the overwhelming amount of food magazines, television shows, websites, blogs, books, etc., the French were obsessed with the culinary arts.

But the French don't just discuss food and consume it, they also get a kick out of actually cooking. The art of selecting ingredients, deciding how they should be prepared and making an effort with presentation adds to the pleasure of eating. There's no better way to experience '*la joie de vivre*', the French passion for all good things in life, than sharing a home-cooked meal with loved ones.

Galette aux pommes de terre et poires avec Roquefort

Potato and pear galette with Roquefort

Jacket potato with melted cheese was one of the best lunches we had at secondary school. You can't beat that melted cheese and potato combo. This is a slightly more sophisticated (but effortless) French *homage* to my humble childhood favourite.

• 4 waxy potatoes, e.g. Maris Peer or Charlotte • 1 firm pear
• 100g Roquefort or another blue cheese

Preheat the oven to 180°C. Peel the potatoes and cut into 2mm-thick slices. On a baking tray lined with baking paper, overlap the potato slices tightly to make 4 rectangles. Peel the pear and cut into small cubes, then sprinkle the cubes over the potatoes and crumble the cheese on top. (Keep the cheese in the middle, otherwise it will drip off the potatoes when it melts.) Bake for about 20 minutes or until the potatoes turn golden brown and crisp around the edges. Serve immediately.

Preparation time: 20 minutes Baking time: 20 minutes

Asperges à la parisienne

Parisian asparagus

The Parisian part of this recipe is the sauce, which also goes by the name of *sauce allemande*. It's basically a *velouté* sauce (see page 270) enriched with egg yolks and a little cream – a great alternative to *hollandaise*.

• a pinch each of salt and sugar • 500g asparagus, trimmed

For the sauce • 30g butter • 30g plain flour • 450ml veal or beef stock, lukewarm
• 2 tablespoons double cream • 2 egg yolks • a couple of drops of lemon juice
• salt and white pepper

To make the sauce, melt the butter in a large pan over a medium heat. Add the flour and beat hard until you have a smooth paste (*roux*). Continue beating until the *roux* begins to have a golden colour. Take off the heat and gradually add the stock, whisking constantly.

Place the pan back over a medium heat and simmer gently for 10 minutes, whisking frequently. If the sauce becomes too thick, whisk in a little more stock.

Meanwhile, bring a large pot of water to a boil. Add the salt and sugar followed by the asparagus and cook for 2 minutes or until the asparagus is tender.

Take the sauce off the heat and whisk in the cream and egg yolks. Season with lemon juice, salt and white pepper.*

Drain the asparagus well and serve immediately, with the sauce spooned over and around.

* The sauce should be used straight away. Do not reheat or the eggs will separate and the sauce will become lumpy.

Preparation: 10 minutes Cooking time: 20 minutes

Endives au jambon

Chicory with ham

People can be put off by *endives* because they sometimes taste bitter. When buying, go for the small ones that are firm and closed. These tend to be less bitter.

• 4 *endives* (chicory) • 4 slices of ham

For the béchamel sauce • 30g butter • 30g plain flour
• 500ml milk, lukewarm • ¼ onion, skin removed • 1 clove
• 1 bay leaf • a pinch each of white pepper and nutmeg • salt

Remove the outer leaves and stems from the *endives* and simmer the *endives* in salted water with a pinch of sugar for 10–15 minutes or until tender.

Meanwhile, make the sauce. Melt the butter in a large pan over a medium heat. Add the flour and beat hard until you have a smooth paste. Take off the heat and leave to cool for 2 minutes, then gradually add the milk, whisking constantly. Place the pan back over a medium heat, add the onion, clove and bay leaf and simmer gently for 10 minutes, whisking frequently. If the sauce becomes too thick, whisk in a little more milk.

Drain the *endives* well. Wrap a slice of ham around each one and place in individual baking dishes (or one large dish if you prefer).

Finish the sauce by removing the onion, clove and bay leaf, then add the pepper and nutmeg and salt to taste. Cover the *endives* with the sauce and put under a hot grill for a couple of minutes or until golden.

Preparation time: 15 minutes Cooking time: 30 minutes

Soufflé au fromage

Cheese soufflé

There are many myths about this French classic, but it mainly comes down to science – it's the heat that makes the bubbles in the egg whites expand when a soufflé is baked. There's no need to stick to the age-old rule of not daring to open the oven while the soufflé is baking. The mixture won't fall unless it actually starts to cool down and, even if it does start to sink, it will rise again. Soufflés and the stories surrounding them are, quite literally, full of hot air.

• 2 tablespoons soft butter, for brushing • 4–6 tablespoons dried breadcrumbs*
• 120g egg whites (roughly 4 medium egg whites) • a pinch of salt
• a couple of drops of lemon juice

For the cheese sauce base • 60g egg yolks (roughly 3 medium egg yolks)
• 1 heaped teaspoon Dijon mustard • a generous pinch each of cayenne pepper, nutmeg and salt
• 20g plain flour • 250ml milk
• 100g Gruyère or mature Comté cheese, or a mature hard cheese of your choice, grated

To make the cheese sauce base, put the egg yolks into a bowl with the mustard, cayenne, nutmeg and salt. Whisk until light and thick, then whisk in the flour. Bring the milk to a boil in a pan and then pour in a slow stream on to the egg mixture, whisking vigorously all the time.

Pour the mixture into a clean pan and whisk continuously over a medium heat, making sure to scrape the side and the bottom of the pan otherwise the mixture will burn. Once the sauce starts to thicken and release a bubble or two, take the pan off the heat.

Stir in the grated cheese and taste for seasoning – the sauce should be slightly overseasoned to allow for the egg whites being added later. Cover the sauce with cling film, patting it down so that it sticks directly on to the sauce. Refrigerate until cool (you can prepare the sauce to this stage up to 2 days in advance).

When you are ready to make the soufflés, preheat the oven to 200°C. Brush 4 ramekins with softened butter, working with upward strokes from the bottom to the top. Check that the entire inside of each dish has been covered with butter before adding a heaped tablespoon of breadcrumbs. Roll and tilt each ramekin so that the breadcrumbs coat the inside evenly.　　　　　　》》》

In a clean glass or metal bowl, whisk the egg whites to stiff peaks with the salt and lemon juice. Beat the cold cheese sauce until smooth and then mix in half the egg whites until fully incorporated. Gently fold in the rest of the egg whites.

Divide the mix between the ramekins and tap the base of each dish on the work surface to ensure that there are no air pockets. Level the surface of each soufflé by pulling a palette knife (or the back edge of a large knife) across the top of the dish, then clean any drips off the outside or they will burn. To help the soufflés rise, run your thumbnail around the top edge of each ramekin to make a groove.

Put the ramekins into the oven immediately and drop the temperature down to 180°C. Bake for 15–20 minutes or until the soufflés have risen by two-thirds of their original size and wobble a little when moved. Serve straightaway.

For a flavoured coating, mix a generous pinch of ground cumin, chilli, dried oregano or finely chopped thyme or rosemary with the breadcrumbs.

Tips for a successful soufflé

• *Butter (using upward brushstrokes) and coat the ramekins properly otherwise the soufflés will stick.*
• *Make sure to separate the eggs carefully. Any traces of egg yolk in the whites will stop the whites whisking into peaks.*
• *Don't use a plastic bowl to whisk the egg whites, as traces of oil or grease from previous use may remain. Any traces of fat will stop the egg whites forming stiff peaks.*
• *Make sure the oven is preheated to the correct temperature. Too cold and the soufflé won't rise, too hot and it will burn on the top before being cooked through.*

Preparation time: 30 minutes   Chilling time: 45 minutes
Baking time: 15–20 minutes

Quenelles lyonnaises au four

Baked Lyon dumplings

France's gastronomic capital is Lyon. The chef Paul Bocuse is based in the area, and two of France's favourite wines, Côtes du Rhône and Beaujolais, come from the region. Then there's the excellent produce (especially *charcuterie*) and the classic dish of dumplings in a creamy sauce. *Quenelles lyonnaises* are not the lead-balloon type of dumplings – whipped-up egg whites make them light and fluffy.

• 400g raw pike fillets,* without skin and bones • 150g soft butter • 300ml milk • 150g plain flour
• 6 eggs, separated • 1 teaspoon salt • a generous pinch each of pepper and nutmeg
• a handful of chopped parsley (optional)

*For the sauce*** • 2 tablespoons dry white wine • 1 teaspoon fish sauce
• 1 tablespoon tomato paste • 150g *crème fraîche* • a generous pinch of cayenne pepper
• a pinch of sugar

Whizz the fish and butter in a blender to make a paste. Bring the milk to a boil, add the flour and beat hard over a low heat until it forms a ball. Leave to cool for 5 minutes, then whizz in the blender with the fish paste and egg yolks until smooth. Whisk the egg whites to soft peaks. Fold the egg whites into the fish paste and season with salt, pepper and nutmeg. Spread the mix over a large tray and cover with cling film. Refrigerate overnight.

The next day, bring a large pot of salted water to a boil and preheat the grill on its highest setting. Using 2 large, deep spoons, form the mixture into *quenelle* shapes. Dip the spoons in warm water between each scoop – this will help stop the mixture sticking.

Lower the dumplings into the boiling water (in batches so as not to overcrowd the pot) and cook for 5 minutes or until they float to the surface. Use a slotted spoon to transfer them to a baking dish, being careful as they're very fragile.

Mix together the ingredients for the sauce, then pour over the dumplings. Put under the grill for 5–10 minutes or until golden and bubbling. If you like, sprinkle parsley on top before serving.

* Pike can be replaced with the fish of your choice, or even chicken breasts.

** The sauce can be replaced with Sauce Béchamel (see page 269) or Sauce Tomate (see page 271), or it can be omitted altogether and the quenelles simply sprinkled with grated mature cheese.

Preparation time: 45 minutes Resting time: overnight
Cooking time: 20 minutes

Blanc-manger aux crevettes et asperges

Prawn and asparagus blancmange

In the Middle Ages, white chicken meat and blanched almonds were used to make *blanc-manger* (*blanc* meaning 'white' and *manger* 'to eat'). The delicate, sweet flavour of prawns goes very nicely with almonds and asparagus in this cool blancmange. Perfect for a hot summer's day.

- 1 tablespoon butter • 350g unshelled large raw prawns • salt • 300g asparagus, ends trimmed
- 400–500ml unsweetened almond milk* • 1 teaspoon fish sauce
- a generous pinch of cayenne pepper • 4 leaves of gelatine (2g each leaf)

Heat the butter in a large, deep frying pan. Add the prawns and cook for 3 minutes or until golden brown. Leave until cool enough to handle, remove the shells and heads and put these back in the pan. Cut the prawns in half lengthways and devein. Place 4 halved prawns, cut-side in, against the wall of each of 6 disposable aluminium cups (5cm diameter x 4cm deep).** Chop the rest into small cubes.

Cut the tips off the asparagus (slightly longer than the depth of the cups) and halve them lengthways. Cut the rest of the asparagus into small cubes. Blanch the asparagus tips and cubes in salted boiling water for 1 minute or until tender but slightly crunchy. Drain and hold under very cold running water for a couple of minutes. Use the tips to line the cups, squeezing them in between the prawns.

Add 300ml almond milk, the fish sauce and cayenne to the prawn shells. Cover and simmer gently for 10 minutes. Pour through a fine sieve into a pan, using the back of a spoon to press out as much liquid as possible. Measure and add more almond milk to make the total 300ml. Taste for salt.

Soak the gelatine in cold water for 10 minutes or until soft. Drain and squeeze out the excess water, then dissolve in the prawn-shell stock, whisking vigorously. (If necessary, heat very gently, stirring until the gelatine dissolves.)

Divide the prawn and asparagus cubes between the lined cups and pour in the stock. Refrigerate for 4 hours or until set.

To serve, run a knife around the top edge of each blancmange, cut a slit on both sides of the foil and peel away the cup.

You can get almond milk in some large supermarkets, health-food shops and online.

** Or use a muffin tin lined with paper cases and remove the blancmanges from the cases to serve.*

Preparation time: 30 minutes Cooking time: 25 minutes
Resting time: 4 hours–overnight

Sabayon aux Saint-Jacques

Scallop sabayon

Sweet sabayons are traditionally seen on dessert menus, but savoury sabayons work equally well as a starter or main course. This recipe is nicely balanced, with the creaminess of the sauce, the natural sweetness of the scallops and a kick from the peppery rocket to round everything off.

• 12 large scallops • 2 tablespoons olive oil • several handfuls of rocket, to garnish

For the sabayon • 4 egg yolks • 100ml dry white wine • a pinch each of sugar and salt

Rinse the scallops under cold running water and then pat dry with paper towels. Set aside.

To make the sabayon, put the egg yolks, wine, sugar and salt into a *bain marie* (a heatproof bowl set over a pot of simmering water), and whisk until thick and foamy, about 10 minutes. To test, draw a figure of eight in the mixture with the whisk – if the figure stays put, then the sabayon is ready. Take the bowl off the pan, cover with a lid or plate and set aside in a warm place while you cook the scallops.

Put the olive oil into a large pan and place over a high heat. Once the oil is smoking hot, lay the scallops in the pan and turn the heat down to medium. Cook the scallops until golden on one side, about 2 minutes. Turn the scallops over, season with salt and continue to cook until the scallops are golden and slightly firm to the touch, a further 2–3 minutes.

Serve the scallops immediately, with the sabayon and a garnish of rocket.

Preparation time: 10 minutes Cooking time: 20 minutes

Crème brûlée aux oignons

Onion crème brûlée

You wouldn't normally think of putting onions in a *crème brûlée*, but surprisingly the two work really well together. Slow, gentle cooking releases the natural sweetness in the onions, which marries well with the creamy base, while the cheese gives the dish a savoury aspect.

• 4 large onions (about 350g) • a knob of butter • 50ml Calvados
• 275ml double cream • 175ml milk • 5 egg yolks
• 50g Gruyère or mature Comté cheese, finely grated • salt and pepper

For the caramel topping • 30g caster sugar • 30g raw cane sugar

Finely slice the onions. Cook the butter and onions in a large pan for 10 minutes until golden brown. Add the Calvados and cook for 10 minutes until it evaporates, stirring often to stop the onions burning. Add the cream and milk. Bring to a boil, remove from the heat and let stand for 30 minutes.

Preheat the oven to 110°C. Pour the cream through a sieve into a pan, and press as much cream out of the onions as possible. Discard the onions. In a large bowl, lightly beat the egg yolks and stir in the cheese. Bring the cream to a boil, then pour slowly over the egg yolks and cheese, stirring constantly. Do not overbeat, as you want to avoid too many bubbles. Season. Divide the mixture between 4 shallow mini gratin dishes (13cm diameter) and place in a deep roasting tin or baking dish.

Place the tin in the oven and pour in lukewarm water to come halfway up the dishes. Bake for 30–40 minutes or until the custards are set around the edges but still slightly loose in the middle. Remove the dishes from the water and leave to cool before covering with cling film (do not let the film touch the custards). Refrigerate for 4 hours or overnight (they will keep for up to 4 days).

Just before serving, make the caramel topping. Uncover the ramekins and check to see if condensation has collected on the custards. If it has, gently place paper towels on the surface to soak up the moisture. Mix the two types of sugar together and sprinkle a nice even layer of sugar over each custard.

Stand the ramekins on a metal tray. Holding a blowtorch* 10–12cm from the sugar and maintaining a slow and even motion, torch the sugar until just before the desired degree of doneness is reached (the sugar will cook for a few seconds after the flame has been removed).

* A blowtorch is best for caramelizing, but if you don't have one, take a large metal spoon and hold it in a gas flame until very hot (it will turn blue, almost black in colour). Place the spoon on the sugar and move it around so that the heat of the spoon caramelizes the sugar.

Preparation time: 30 minutes Resting time: 4 hours–overnight
Cooking time: 1 hour

Choucroute garnie

Alsatian pork, crackling and sausages with a 'speedy' sauerkraut

A winter warmer from Alsace. Originally a one-pot stew made with fresh, cured and smoked pork, I've broken it down into three components: a 'speedy' sauerkraut with a crunch factor, a smoky bacon broth and the meat. I'm a big fan of a crisp crackling, so I put everything in the oven rather than cook it as a stew: the flavours are the same, but the textures are different.

• 500g boned pork belly with fat and skin* • salt, for sprinkling
• 4 frankfurters or other smoked sausages • 4 thick slices of smoked bacon

For the bouillon • 200g piece of smoked bacon • 500ml cold water

For the speedy sauerkraut • 10 juniper berries • 100ml dry white wine, ideally from Alsace
• 400ml cold water • 100g sugar • 35g salt • 250ml white wine vinegar
• 500g hard white cabbage, finely shredded

Put the smoked bacon in a pot with the water, cover and bring to a boil. Simmer gently for 30 minutes. Strain through a very fine sieve. (This can be made in advance and kept in the fridge overnight.)

To make the sauerkraut, put the juniper berries into a dry pan and heat. Add the wine and reduce to a couple of tablespoons, then add the water and boil. Add the sugar, salt and wine vinegar and stir over a low heat until the sugar dissolves. Pour over the cabbage in a plastic container, let cool, then cover and refrigerate for 1–4 hours. (It will keep in an airtight container in the fridge for up to a week. The longer it marinates, the less crunchy it will be, but it will still be delicious.)

Preheat the oven to 250°C, or its hottest setting, and line a roasting tray with baking paper. Pat the skin of the pork dry with paper towels** before sprinkling and rubbing with salt. Roast the pork for 10 minutes, then turn the heat down to 180°C and roast for a further hour before adding the sausages and smoked bacon slices. Roast for a further 30 minutes, shaking the tray and turning the sausages and bacon halfway. If the pork skin isn't crisping, turn the heat up to 220°C.

To serve, bring the *bouillon* to a boil and slice the crispy pork into 4 portions. Place the pork on individual plates with a slice of bacon, a sausage and a spoonful of sauerkraut, then pour over a ladle of the hot *bouillon*. Serve with a Dijon or grainy mustard, and boiled or roasted small new potatoes.

* The skin must be scored. Ask your butcher, or use a very sharp knife. Don't cut through to the meat.

*** **Pourquoi?** The drier the skin, the crisper the crackling.*

Preparation time: 40 minutes   Cooking time: 2¼ hours

Bouillon de cassoulet avec des boulettes de canard et saucisse de Toulouse

Cassoulet soup with duck and Toulouse sausage dumplings

I first encountered *cassoulet* in jars at the supermarket, and I quickly discovered it's a dish seen more in jars than bubbling away on the kitchen stove (it's quite time-consuming to make). This recipe has the key *cassoulet* ingredients: duck, Toulouse sausage, tomato, smoked bacon and white beans, but there's no stewing for hours. Instead of being a heavy dish, my *cassoulet* has a light touch with its *bouillon* base and duck and sausage dumplings.

- 300g piece of smoked bacon • 50g sun-dried tomatoes, rinsed well if marinated in oil
- 30g dried *cèpes* or *porcini* • 1.75 litres cold water • 2 tablespoons tomato paste
- 1 teaspoon brown sugar • 1 teaspoon salt • ½ teaspoon pepper
- 250g tin white beans (e.g. *haricots blancs*, *cannellini*), drained and rinsed
- 2 carrots, thinly sliced into rounds • sprigs of parsley, to garnish

For the dumplings • 300g duck breast, fat and skin removed • 1 clove of garlic, chopped
• ½ onion, chopped • ½ teaspoon pepper • 300g Toulouse sausages, skinned

Put the bacon, sun-dried tomatoes and dried mushrooms into a large pot with the water. Bring to a boil, cover and simmer for 30 minutes. Take off the heat, remove the bacon, tomatoes and mushrooms and discard. Whisk in the tomato paste and add the sugar, salt and pepper. Taste and adjust seasoning. (This *bouillon* can be kept in an airtight container in the fridge for up to 2 days.)*

To make the dumplings, roughly chop the duck and whizz in an electric blender with the garlic, onion and pepper until the same texture as sausagemeat. Using your hands, combine this mixture with the Toulouse sausage, then take about 2 tablespoons of the mixture at a time and roll into small balls. (These can be kept in an airtight container in the fridge for up to 2 days.)*

To serve, bring the *bouillon* to a simmer and add the beans and carrots. Simmer for 5 minutes (don't cook for too long or the beans may disintegrate). Meanwhile, heat a large non-stick frying pan until hot. Place half the dumplings in the pan and cook for 8–10 minutes, shaking the pan once in a while to stop them sticking. Remove and repeat with the remaining dumplings. Divide the dumplings between soup bowls, pour the soup over them and garnish with parsley.

*Both the *bouillon* and the uncooked dumplings can be frozen for up to 2 months. Defrost the dumplings for a couple of hours before frying.

Preparation time: 30 minutes Cooking time: about 1 hour

Bouillabaisse

Provençal fish stew

This quintessential Provençal dish from Marseille combines the best local seafood with the flavours of Provence: fennel seeds, saffron and orange. A simple dish has evolved into something much more elaborate, and nowadays a *bouillabaisse* may include three types of fish and three types of shellfish. In Marseille the stock is served as a soup with *rouille* and bread, followed by the fish and vegetables. I'm going back to its roots here, omitting the large assortment of fish, keeping it simple but retaining the original flavours. By using fillets instead of whole fish, it makes the dish less daunting for guests who fear the 'fish bone in throat' situation.

- 400g fish fillets of your choice (I use hake, pollack and salmon), cut into large chunks
- 500g mussels, cleaned • 500g prawns, no shells • salt and pepper
- a couple of spring onions, finely sliced

For the rouille • 2 cloves of garlic • 1 egg yolk
- a pinch each of cayenne pepper and saffron threads • 250ml sunflower oil • salt

For the soup base • 4 tablespoons olive oil • 1 onion, finely chopped
- 4 cloves of garlic, crushed to a paste • 2 tablespoons tomato paste • 2 star anise
- 1 teaspoon fennel seeds • 1 bay leaf • 3 sprigs of thyme • pared zest of 1 unwaxed orange
- a pinch of chilli powder • 1 teaspoon saffron threads • 1 stick of celery, finely sliced
- 1 bulb of fennel, finely sliced • 3 large tomatoes, roughly chopped • 150ml dry white wine
- 1 litre fish stock • juice of 1 orange (50ml)

To make the *rouille*, crush the garlic cloves to a fine paste in a large bowl. Add the egg yolk, cayenne and saffron. Drizzle the oil slowly into the bowl, whisking hard (you can use an electric whisk). Taste for salt, cover and refrigerate until you are ready to serve.*

To make the soup base, heat the olive oil in a large pot and add the onion, garlic, tomato paste, star anise, fennel seeds, bay leaf, thyme, orange zest, chilli powder, saffron, celery, fennel and tomatoes. Cook until the onion is soft, then add the wine and reduce by half. Pour in the stock and orange juice, bring to a rapid boil and cook for 10 minutes. Lower the heat and add the seafood, then cover and simmer gently for 5 minutes, shaking the pan a few times. Taste for seasoning before serving sprinkled with the spring onions. Hand the *rouille* round in a bowl, with crusty bread.

*The rouille *is best made on the day of serving, because of the raw egg yolks, but you can make the soup base the day before as this will give the flavours time to develop. When ready to serve, simply bring to a boil and throw in the seafood.*

Preparation time: 30 minutes Cooking time: 25 minutes

Poisson meunière

Fish with lemon and brown butter sauce

Meunière translates as 'miller's wife', referring to the flour used to dredge the fish before it is cooked. This acts as a protective barrier, preventing the delicate flesh from drying out. I use lemon sole for my *meunière* (Dover sole is just too expensive), but why not try other fish such as Pacific halibut or even trout? If you have a reputable local fishmonger, have a chat with him to see what he recommends. A key factor in making this dish delicious is the brown butter and lemon sauce, although the capers and chopped parsley make a tasty addition too.

- 2 fillets of lemon sole (about 150g each), skin removed
- 3 tablespoons plain flour • ½ teaspoon salt • a generous pinch of pepper
- 1½ tablespoons sunflower oil • 45g butter, cut into cubes • juice of ½ lemon
- 1 tablespoon chopped parsley • 1 tablespoon small capers (optional)

Check the fish for small bones and use tweezers to pull out any that you find.

Mix the flour with the salt and pepper and spread out over a large plate. Pat the fish fillets in the flour so they are evenly coated, and shake off any excess.

Heat the oil in a large frying pan over a high heat, When the oil is smoking hot, place the fish fillets fleshy-side down in the pan and lower the heat to medium. Cook for 1–2 minutes on one side until golden, then turn the fillets over and cook for a further 1–2 minutes until the second side is golden.* Place the fish on a warmed plate and cover with aluminium foil.

Wipe the pan with paper towels and return to a medium heat. Add the cubes of butter and heat until they melt and become light brown, then turn off the heat and add the lemon juice (stand back a little as it will splutter). Add the parsley and capers (if using), and swirl the contents of the pan around. Return the fish to the pan, spoon over the juices and serve immediately.

* Flat fish fillets need only 1–2 minutes cooking on each side. If you're cooking thicker slices or fillets from a fish like trout (2–3cm thick), then 3–4 minutes on each side should be fine.

Preparation time: 10 minutes   Cooking time: 10 minutes

Brochettes au coq au vin

Coq au vin on skewers

Cockerel stewed in red wine for several hours is traditional *coq au vin*. I thought I'd shake that on its head and make a barbecue version with a red wine dipping sauce.

• 750g boned chicken legs, with skin on* • 150g *lardons* or cubes of smoked bacon
• 2 large carrots, cut into large chunks • 8 small new potatoes
• 8 small button onions, peeled and left whole • 1 tablespoon red wine vinegar
• 1 tablespoon cornflour • 1 tablespoon sugar • salt and pepper
• 8 small button mushrooms, brushed or peeled • 1 tablespoon olive oil

For the marinade • 2 cloves of garlic, finely chopped • 1 onion, finely chopped
• a knob of butter • 4 small sprigs of thyme • 3 bay leaves • 500ml red wine

8 barbecue skewers — if they're bamboo, soak them in water for at least an hour before using

To make the marinade, fry the garlic and onion in the butter until golden brown. Add the thyme and bay leaves and cook for a further minute before adding the wine. Bring to a boil and simmer for 10 minutes. Leave to cool. Cut the chicken into large chunks, place in a large plastic container with the *lardons* and add the cold marinade. Cover and marinate in the fridge for at least 4 hours (best overnight).

Lift the chicken and *lardons* out of the marinade, then strain through a sieve. Measure 300ml marinade, pour it into a pan and set aside. Put the carrots, potatoes and onions into a large pan of cold salted water and bring to a boil. Parboil for 5 minutes, then drain the vegetables into a sieve and hold under cold running water for 2 minutes. Leave to cool.

Make the dipping sauce. On a high heat, reduce the marinade by half before adding the vinegar. Mix the cornflour to a thin paste with some water, whisk into the sauce and boil for 5 minutes or until the consistency of double cream. Add the sugar and season with salt and pepper. Cover with cling film, pressing it down in direct contact with the sauce. Keep the sauce warm until needed.

Thread the chicken on to the skewers, alternating with the *lardons*, parboiled vegetables and mushrooms. Brush with olive oil before cooking on the barbecue (or indoors on a griddle pan) for around 5 minutes, turning regularly. To check the chicken is cooked, cut a piece open — the juices should run clear, not red or pink. Serve with the sauce (reheated in a pan or microwave if necessary).

* Chicken legs have more flavour and tend to be juicier than breast, or you could use boneless chicken thighs (skin on) instead. Breast meat will be fine too, as long as you are careful not to overcook it.

Preparation time: 1 hour Resting time: 4 hours–overnight
Cooking time: 20 minutes

Poulet au citron et lavande

Lemon and lavender chicken

The lavender fields in Provence are a spectacular sight, but if you can't make it to see them I think that using a little lavender in your cooking is probably the next best thing. In moderation, lavender tastes delicious in both savoury and sweet dishes, but don't use too much or they'll start tasting like granny's soap.

• 1 chicken, jointed into 8–10 pieces • a generous pinch of salt

For the marinade • 2 tablespoons dried lavender • 4 tablespoons olive oil
• 4 tablespoons lavender honey or plain runny honey • 2 sprigs of thyme
• finely grated zest and juice of 1 unwaxed lemon

To make the marinade, crush the lavender using either a mortar and pestle or a rolling pin. Put the crushed lavender into a large bowl with the oil, honey, thyme, lemon zest and juice. Mix well.

Place the chicken pieces in a large plastic container. Pour the marinade over the chicken and make sure all the pieces are well coated. Cover and leave to marinate for 30 minutes (or up to 4 hours).

When you are ready to cook, preheat the oven to 200°C. Put the chicken and marinade into a roasting tin and sprinkle with a generous pinch of salt. Roast the chicken for 45 minutes, turning the pieces over halfway. To check if the chicken is done, pierce the thickest part of the flesh with a skewer – the juices should run clear, not red or pink.

Serve the chicken with the cooking juices poured over and around. A crisp green salad and some boiled new potatoes are a great match for this summery dish.

Preparation time: 10 minutes Resting time: 30 minutes–4 hours
Cooking time: 45 minutes

Poulet aux champignons avec une sauce au vin blanc

Chicken and mushrooms in a white wine sauce

You can't go wrong with this classic, and the white wine sauce is great to know. You can flavour it with fresh herbs, such as parsley, tarragon or dill, and use it with many other ingredients besides chicken and mushrooms. I like it with poached fish or vegetables (especially leeks and boiled potatoes), and it's also an easy way to make something tasty out of leftovers – it's really good poured over roast chicken or turkey.

• a knob of butter • 500g chicken or turkey breast, cut into chunks
• 250g button mushrooms, brushed or peeled, then sliced
• a handful of finely chopped tarragon or parsley

For the sauce • 30g butter • 30g plain flour • 450ml chicken stock, lukewarm
• 125ml dry white wine • 4 tablespoons double cream • 1 teaspoon lemon juice • salt and pepper

To make the sauce, melt the butter in a large pan over a medium heat. Add the flour and beat hard until you have a smooth paste (*roux*). Continue to beat until the *roux* begins to have a golden colour. Take off the heat and gradually add the stock, whisking constantly.

Place the pan back over a medium heat and simmer gently for 10 minutes, whisking frequently to ensure none of the sauce burns on the bottom of the pan. If the sauce becomes too thick, whisk in a little more stock.

Add the wine and continue simmering for 10 minutes, then take off the heat and whisk in the cream and lemon juice. Taste for seasoning.

While the sauce is simmering, cook the chicken. Melt the knob of butter in a large frying pan until sizzling, add the chicken and fry for a few minutes until golden. Add the mushrooms and fry for a further 5 minutes or until the chicken is cooked through.

To serve, mix the sauce with the chicken and mushrooms and sprinkle with some fresh tarragon. Serve with steamed rice or pasta.

Preparation time: 15 minutes Cooking time: 30 minutes

Blanquette de veau

Veal ragout

The French like their one-pot wonders – *coq au vin, boeuf bourguignon* and *pot-au-feu*, for instance. *Blanquette de veau* is another 'throw it all in the pot' type of dish, and it's actually simpler than many other stews as there's no browning of the meat to be done – hence the name *blanquette*.

Normally some of the stock is combined with egg yolks and cream to make a rich white sauce, but as this dish should be about keeping work to a minimum, why bother when you can make a pretty mean sauce with just a pot of *crème frâiche* (full-fat, please), some orange zest and black pepper? My *caviste* (wine guy) gave me the tip of adding orange zest to the stew.

• 1kg piece of veal belly (breast) with skin • 10 button onions, peeled
• 6 carrots, cut into chunks • 1 bay leaf • 1 sprig of rosemary • 1 sprig of thyme
• 10 peppercorns • a bunch of parsley stalks
• pared zest of 2 unwaxed oranges • 10 button mushrooms, brushed or peeled • salt

For the sauce • 100g crème fraîche • finely grated zest of 1 unwaxed orange • salt and pepper

Preheat the oven to 160°C. Place the meat in a large ovenproof pot with all the other ingredients except the mushrooms. Pour in cold water until the meat and vegetables are submerged, then cover the pot with its lid, place in the oven and cook for 2 hours.

Take the pot out of the oven. Remove the meat, onions and carrots from the stock and set aside. Tip the contents of the pot into a very fine sieve or coffee filter set over a bowl and let the stock run through (to remove any impurities).

Pour the stock into a clean pot and add the meat, onions, carrots and mushrooms. Simmer gently for about 5 minutes or until the mushrooms are cooked. Taste for salt.

To make the sauce, mix the *crème fraîche* with the orange zest and season with salt and pepper to taste.

Lift the meat out of the stock and cut into slices. Serve each person with a slice of veal, a spoonful of vegetables, a ladleful of stock and a large helping of the sauce. Boiled potatoes, rice or even pasta go nicely with this dish.

Preparation time: 20 minutes Cooking time: 2–2½ hours

Boeuf bourguignon avec des quenelles de baguettes

Burgundy beef with baguette dumplings

Each region in France uses their own local red wine for this dish, so you don't need to use a bottle of Burgundy. The idea of the dumplings came to me when I started accumulating odd ends of leftover *baguettes*. They make a great alternative to potatoes, as well as soaking up the juices from the stew.

• 900g beef shin or stewing beef, cut into 6 large chunks • 2 tablespoons plain flour
• 2 tablespoons vegetable oil • 150g *lardons* or cubes of smoked bacon
• 10 button onions or shallots, peeled • 2 cloves of garlic, crushed until flat • 1 bay leaf
• a bunch of parsley stalks • 1 sprig of thyme • 1 sprig of rosemary • 3 cloves
• 10 peppercorns, crushed • 500ml red wine • 300ml water • 1 tablespoon tomato paste
• a pinch of sugar • 10 chestnut mushrooms • chopped parsley, to garnish

For the dumplings • 200g stale *baguette* or other bread (crust included) • 250ml milk
• a pinch of nutmeg • salt and pepper • a handful of chopped parsley • 1 egg
• 1–2 tablespoons plain flour • a knob of butter, for frying

Preheat the oven to 150°C. Dust each piece of meat with flour. Heat the oil in a large casserole over a high heat and fry the meat in batches until browned. Remove each batch, then fry the *lardons*, onions, garlic, herbs and spices in the same pan until golden brown. Return the meat to the pan and add the wine, water, tomato paste and sugar. Scrape up the caramelized bits – they will add flavour. Cover, place in the oven and cook for 3 hours or until the meat is tender and almost falling apart.*

Cut the baguette into small cubes and place in a bowl. Bring the milk to a boil and pour over. Stir so that the milk is absorbed evenly, then cover and leave for 15 minutes. Season with nutmeg, salt and pepper, stir in the chopped parsley and egg, and mix in 1 tablespoon flour. If the mix is too wet (it should be moist and only slightly sticky), add a second spoon of flour. Wet your hands a little to help stop the dough sticking to them, then make 12–14 dumplings (smaller than a golf ball).*

About 20 minutes before the stew is ready, add the mushrooms and season with salt to taste. Heat a knob of butter in a large frying pan and fry the dumplings on a medium heat for 5 minutes or until golden brown and crisp, then drain. Garnish the stew with parsley and serve with the dumplings.

* Make the stew the day before to give the flavours time to develop. Add the mushrooms before gently reheating (no boiling). The dumplings can be kept in an airtight container in the fridge for 2 hours.

Preparation time: 45 minutes Cooking time: 3 hours

'One of the best things about Paris is being able to shop at small independent grocery shops that are still affordable. I'm lucky to have a great family-run butcher in my neighbourhood. They have a brilliant selection of meat and are always happy to give you some advice on how to cook it'

Mini chevreuil en croûte

Mini Venison Wellington

I've made countless *boeufs en croûte* with the traditional mushroom filling and puff pastry, but I've found the recipe is equally good with venison, red onions and Armagnac, whose caramel notes work particularly well with the natural sweetness in the onions.

- 4 venison (or beef) steaks, each about 175g and 2cm thick • salt and pepper
- 3 large red onions, finely sliced • 2 knobs of butter • a pinch of sugar
- a generous pinch of salt • 2 tablespoons Armagnac
- 500g puff pastry or croissant dough*, cut into quarters • 3 tablespoons Dijon mustard
- 1 egg mixed with 2 tablespoons water, for the eggwash

Place a large non-stick frying pan over the highest possible heat. Season the meat all over with salt and pepper. When the pan is smoking hot, put in the steaks and sear for 30 seconds on each side. Remove and set aside for later. In the same pan over a medium heat, gently cook the onions with the butter, sugar and salt for 20 minutes until caramelized and soft. Add the Armagnac and cook, stirring occasionally, for 10 minutes until the onions become drier. Leave to cool for 10 minutes before blending to a smooth paste. Refrigerate for about an hour until cold (or freeze for speed).

Between 2 sheets of baking paper, roll out one-quarter of the pastry to a ½cm-thick rectangle. Cut in half widthways to make 2 squares slightly larger than the steaks. Repeat with the remaining pastry to make 8 squares. Preheat the oven to 200°C and line a baking tray with baking paper.

Brush some mustard all over a piece of steak, then place the steak in the middle of a square of pastry. Top the steak with a heaped tablespoon of the onion mix, brush eggwash around the pastry edges and cover with another pastry square. Press the edges to seal, then trim the excess pastry to leave a 1cm border and crimp with a fork. Repeat with the other pieces of pastry and the remaining 3 steaks. Cut a little cross in the top of each parcel and brush the pastry with eggwash. Place the parcels on the prepared tray and bake for 12 minutes for medium-rare meat.** Remove from the oven, cover with aluminium foil and leave to rest for 5 minutes before serving.

* I order puff pastry and croissant dough from the bakery if I haven't time to make it, or even buy them at the supermarket, picking one made with all butter (no palm oil, emulsifers, additives, etc.).

** If you have a meat thermometer, push it into the cross in the top of one of the parcels to check the internal temperature of the meat. 55–59°C medium rare (red in the centre), 60–66°C medium (pink in the centre), 67–71°C well done (grey-brown throughout).

Preparation time: 30 minutes Resting time: 1 hour
Cooking time: 45 minutes

Pot-au-feu de joue de boeuf

Beef cheek 'pot-on-the-fire'

Almost every cuisine has a famous one-pot dish that benefits from sitting on the stove for several hours. The French are pretty clever with their *pot-au-feu*, making a simple one pot work as two courses. The broth makes a dark and delicious *consommé* starter, then the meat and vegetables are served as a main course with the traditional condiments of mustard, *cornichons* and salt.

Pop the pot on the stove mid-morning and it'll be perfect for dinner. It's actually even better made a day in advance and gently warmed up just before serving. Who said you had to slave away in the kitchen to be a French domestic goddess?

• 2–3 beef cheeks* (total weight 1.5kg), fat removed and each cheek cut in half
• 1kg oxtail or veal knuckles, chopped • 1 bouquet garni (2 bay leaves, 2 sprigs of thyme,
6 sprigs of parsley, 10 peppercorns, 5 cloves)
• 2 onions, quartered with skin left on • 2 sticks of celery • 2 carrots • 1 turnip, halved

To finish • 4 carrots, quartered • 3 turnips, quartered
• 10 button onions, peeled and left whole, or 2 regular onions, quartered
• salt and pepper • 1 bay leaf, to garnish

Put the meat and bones into a large pot, cover with cold water and bring slowly to a simmer. Drain and discard the water, then rinse the bones, meat and pot with cold water to remove the impurities.

Place the bones and meat back in the clean pot, cover with cold water again and bring slowly to a 'barely-there' simmer. Skim off any scum that comes to the surface and then add the bouquet garni, onions, celery, carrots and turnip. Continue to simmer very gently (around 80°C), uncovered, until the meat is tender and almost falling apart. This can take between 6 and 8 hours. Make sure the meat is always submerged, topping up with cold water if necessary.

Once the meat is cooked, remove it from the broth and pour the contents of the pan into a fine sieve or coffee filter set over a bowl. Discard the vegetables and anything else that doesn't filter through.

To finish, pour the broth into a clean pot and add the meat and fresh vegetables (carrots, turnips and onions). Simmer for 30 minutes or until the vegetables are cooked. Taste for seasoning and garnish with a bay leaf.

At the table, spoon the meat and vegetables into bowls with a little of the broth, and hand round condiments (French mustard, *cornichons*, coarse sea salt), plus bowls of Spicy green sauce and Cream sauce (see page 200).

»»»

To serve the *pot-au-feu* the next day:

After cooking and separating the broth and meat, refrigerate them in separate airtight containers overnight. The next day, the broth will have set as a jelly with the impurities settled as a dark layer at the bottom. Put the top, clear part of the jelly into a pot with the meat and fresh vegetables and heat gently until the jelly has melted. Top up with a little water if needed to cover everything and simmer gently for 30 minutes or until the vegetables are cooked. Taste for seasoning. This technique will make a clearer broth.

* *If you want to use the traditional cuts of beef such as rib, shoulder or leg, ask the butcher to tie the meat with a string (to stop it from falling apart). Poultry, game or lamb on the bone can be used instead of the beef cheeks and oxtail. Cooking time will vary depending on the size and type of meat, i.e. a whole chicken, jointed into 8–10 pieces, will take 1½ hours (plus 30 minutes for the fresh vegetables). Lamb shanks will take 3–4 hours, depending on their size (plus 30 minutes for the fresh vegetables).*

Preparation time: 30 minutes   Cooking time: 6½–8½ hours

Spicy green sauce

- ½ long red chilli, deseeded • 1 clove of garlic • ½ bunch of curly parsley (stalks included)
- 5 tablespoons red wine vinegar • 5 tablespoons olive oil • 1 teaspoon sugar • salt (optional)

Blend all the ingredients together (except salt) until you have a thick paste. Taste and season with salt, if necessary. Refrigerate until needed (can be kept in an airtight container in the fridge for several days).

Cream sauce

- 250g *crème fraîche* • 10 *cornichons*, finely chopped • 1 teaspoon Dijon mustard
- 1 teaspoon sugar • 2 tablespoons lemon juice • salt (optional)

Mix all the ingredients together (except salt). Taste and season with salt, if necessary. Refrigerate until needed (can be kept in an airtight container in the fridge for several days).

Fajitas de pot-au-feu

French beef stew fajitas

Fajitas de pot-au-feu may not sound like a French recipe, but in essence it is – *pot-au-feu* leftovers are wrapped in tortillas with the addition of some crunchy veg. I make my own tortillas, but you can buy them ready-made at the supermarket.

• 3 tablespoons olive oil • 200g leftover meat from *Pot-au-feu* (see page 199) or leftover roast meat, shredded with a fork • 2 carrots, shaved into thin strips or grated • ¼ red cabbage, shredded

For the tortillas • 300g plain flour • 1 teaspoon baking powder • 1 teaspoon salt • 200ml milk, lukewarm • 2 tablespoons vegetable oil

To serve • Cream sauce and Spicy green sauce (see page 200)

To make the tortillas, mix the flour, baking powder and salt together in a bowl. Add the milk and oil and use your fingertips to mix the ingredients together. Once the dough has formed a sticky ball, turn it out on to a floured surface and knead for 5 minutes. It will become less sticky the more you knead it, so don't use too much flour at the beginning. Grease a bowl with some oil before placing the dough into it and covering. Leave to rest for 20 minutes.

Put a large non-stick frying pan over a medium to high heat. Divide the dough into 6 small balls, and dust your work surface and rolling pin with a little flour. Roll out a ball of dough into a small, thin disc (roughly 15cm in diameter and 2mm thick).

Place the tortilla in the pan and cook for about a minute until golden on each side. Repeat the process to make 6 tortillas in total, then wrap the tortillas in aluminium foil and keep them warm in the oven until you are ready to serve.

Put 1 tablespoon of the olive oil into a large pan and set on a medium heat. Add the shredded meat and cook for several minutes until hot and slightly caramelized. Meanwhile, put the carrots and cabbage in a bowl and toss togther with the remaining 2 tablespoons olive oil.

To serve, spread a teaspoonful of cream sauce over each tortilla. Add some meat and vegetables, and top with green sauce. Alternatively, set bowls of each ingredient and the tortillas on the table for everyone to help themselves.

Preparation time: 20 minutes
Resting time: 20 minutes Cooking time: 15 minutes

Steak et frites de légumes racines

Steak and root-vegetable fries

Juicy steak with crisp fries: a match made in heaven. There are different cuts – *entrecôte* (rib-eye), *filet* (fillet), *bavette* (skirt), *rumsteack* (rump), *faux-filet* (sirloin) – but the method stays the same (first sear and then finish in the oven) unless the meat is less than 1cm thick or is to be served rare. So there's not much to it, apart from letting the steak rest after cooking – this will make a world of difference.

• 1 rib-eye steak (about 500g) • salt and pepper

For the fries • 25g ground almonds • 2 tablespoons sunflower oil • salt and pepper
• 1 sweet potato, cut into thin strips • 1 parsnip, cut into thin strips
• 1 large carrot, cut into thin strips

To make the fries, preheat the oven to 200°C. In a large bowl, mix together the ground almonds, oil, ½ teaspoon salt and some pepper. Toss the vegetables in the mix and then spread them out in a single layer over a baking tray. Bake for 30 minutes or until crisp, shaking the tray halfway through.

Season the steak with salt and pepper on both sides. Heat a non-stick frying pan on a high heat. When it is so hot you can't hold your hand over it, sear the steak in the pan for 2 minutes on each side. Depending how you want it done,* put the steak in the oven with the fries for between 5 and 10 minutes. Once the steak is cooked, wrap in foil and leave to rest on a warm plate for 10 minutes.

To serve, unwrap the steak and cut in half. Serve straight away with the fries, and with mustard or *Sauce tartare* (see page 273) if you like.

* There are roughly four degrees of 'doneness'. To test whether it is done to your liking, press your finger on the steak and gauge how it feels (see below), or you can use a meat thermometer.

Rare – *bleu:* pinch your thumb and index finger together. Feel the fleshy part of your palm below the thumb and this should have the firmness of a rare steak. Sear only – there is no need to finish cooking in the oven. Colour: very red. Meat temperature: 52–55°C.

Medium rare – *à point:* as for rare above, but with your thumb and middle finger together. Sear, then finish cooking in the oven. Colour: red in the centre. Meat temperature 55–60°C.

Medium – *cuit:* as for rare above, but with your ring finger and thumb together. Sear, then finish cooking in the oven. Colour: pink in the centre. Meat temperature 60–66°C.

Well-done – *bien cuit:* as for rare above, but with your little finger and thumb together. Sear, then finish cooking in the oven. Colour: grey-brown throughout. Meat temperature 67–71°C.

Preparation time: 20 minutes Cooking time: 30 minutes

Canard à l'Orangina

Duck with fizzy orange

When I was invited to a dinner hosted by the chef Jean-François Piège, he described how his previous elaborate style of cooking at the Hôtel de Crillon had evolved into something a lot more simple and homely at his current restaurant in the Hôtel Thoumieux. He told an amusing story of how his wife wanted duck *à l'orange* for Sunday supper and all he could find at his local corner shop was Orangina, so he used it to make a sauce for the duck. I'm not sure exactly how he made his *canard à l'Orangina*, but here's my version.

• 4 duck legs • 100ml fizzy orange • 2 tablespoons Cointreau
• a pinch of salt • 1 teaspoon red wine vinegar • 4 oranges, cut into segments

For the marinade • finely grated zest and juice of 1 unwaxed orange • 1 tablespoon olive oil
• ½ teaspoon ground cumin • 1 teaspoon salt

To make the marinade, mix together the orange zest and juice with the olive oil, cumin and salt.

Rub the marinade over the duck legs and leave to marinate for a minimum of an hour (or in the fridge overnight).

Preheat the oven to 170°C. Put the duck legs with the marinade into a roasting tray and cook for 1 hour. Halfway through cooking, baste the duck with some of the pan juices.

Fifteen minutes before serving, pour the fizzy orange and Cointreau into a large frying pan, place on a high heat and simmer until reduced by half. Stir in the salt and wine vinegar before adding the orange segments. Simmer for a further 5 minutes.

Serve the duck legs hot, with the oranges and fizzy orange sauce. A simple watercress or wild rocket salad works well with this dish.

Preparation time: 20 minutes Resting time: 1 hour–overnight
Cooking time: 1 hour

Magret de canard avec salade d'endives et framboises

Duck breast with an endive and raspberry salad

There's a bit of a colour theme going on with this dish – red raspberries and *endives* with pink from the duck – but that's not the reason why I put these ingredients together. The tartness of the raspberries and the bitterness of the *endives* are divine with the gamey taste of the duck.

- 2 large duck breasts *(magrets)*, skin on • salt and pepper
- 4 small red *endives* (chicory) or *radicchio*
- 8 tablespoons extra virgin olive oil • 4 tablespoons raspberry vinegar
- 1 punnet of raspberries

Trim some of the fat off the duck breasts and score the skin. Rub salt and pepper on both sides of the breasts.

Place a large frying pan over a high heat. When the pan is so hot that you can't hold your hand over it, place the duck breasts, skin-side down, in the pan and turn the heat down to medium-high. Fry the breasts for 4–5 minutes on each side or until golden brown and cooked to your liking (see *Steak et frites*, page 207). You may want to drain off some of the fat while cooking, but don't throw it away – duck fat is excellent for roasting potatoes. Once the duck is cooked to your liking, remove the breasts from the pan, wrap them in aluminium foil and leave to rest on a warm plate for 10 minutes.

Meanwhile, wash and dry the salad leaves. If they are big, cut them into smaller pieces. Put the leaves into a large bowl and sprinkle with the olive oil, raspberry vinegar and seasoning to taste. Toss well, then scatter over 4 plates with the raspberries.

Carve the duck into very thin slices and divide between the plates. Serve with some crusty bread to mop up the juices, or with diced boiled potatoes that have been pan-fried in some of the duck fat.

Preparation time: 20 minutes   Resting time: 10 minutes
Cooking time: 8–10 minutes

LES AMANDES LE SUCRE LA FRAISE LA GOUSSE DE VANILLE L'ORANGE LA MARYSE

 LA FARINE LE LAIT LE ROMARIN LE CAFÉ LE BLANC D'ŒUF LE JAUNE D'ŒUF LES CERISES

 LE ROULEAU À PÂTISSERIE

 LA POIRE

Sweet Treats

Gourmandises

 LA CRÈME CHANTILLY

 LA FARINE

 LE FOUET LE ROULEAU À PÂTISSERIE LA GOUSSE DE VANILLE LE ROMARIN LE SUCRE LA RHUBARBE

 LES AMANDES L'ORANGE LA MARYSE LA FRAISE LES TOMATES CERISES LE THÉ

I've met quite a few foreigners who moved to Paris because they fell madly in love with a Frenchie. But it wasn't a charming Frenchman sweeping me off my feet that made me pack my bags and cross the channel.

While window-shopping on a school trip to Paris, I fell under the spell of French cakes in all sorts of shapes and sizes. Sugar-coated, they glistened in the windows of the *pâtisseries* with the sweet promise of delighting my tastebuds. I was quite literally licking the windows, as in the French idiom for window-shopping: *faire du lèche-vitrine*.

Not content with eating them, I wanted to know the secrets of making them. So I enrolled on a *pâtisserie* course at Le Cordon Bleu, Paris. Before I was even let anywhere close to the kitchen, I was drilled to say '*Oui, chef*'. Several hundred eggs and tons of sugar, flour and butter later, I had learned how to whip up some of the sweet culinary delights I had seen in the *pâtisserie* windows.

One thing I learned quickly was that these recipes have to be followed to a 'T', unlike cooking, where you can follow your own taste. Weighing your ingredients in most cases is an absolute must. *Pâtisserie* is a science. Too much of a certain ingredient can cause total chaos with the end result. The ingredients used in French *pâtisserie* aren't that many: butter, sugar, eggs and flour usually suffice to create something that will tantalize everyone's tastebuds.

French *pâtisserie* is founded on key recipes and techniques. Certain recipes like *Crème pâtissière* or shortcrust pastry are considered building blocks. Once you've mastered a few, you can easily adapt them to make a broad range of other desserts.

This chapter covers a wide range of French desserts: some are simple and others a little more complicated. The more complex desserts are broken down into several shorter recipes (which in some cases can be used on their own). Don't be put off by the length. Take your time to read through the recipe, set up your equipment and weigh your ingredients before you start making the dessert — just a few tips I learned at culinary school. With a little practice, you'll be able to use some of the key recipes to make your own French-inspired creations.

Café Gourmand

This has to be one of the best ideas to appear on bistro and restaurant menus. I've always had a hard time making up my mind what to order for dessert, but with *Café Gourmand* you get three mini versions instead of having to choose just one. It's the perfect solution for my indecisive self.

To make all three mini desserts you will need one quantity of the *Crème pâtissière* recipe (see page 274), which you should make in advance and chill in the fridge. The mousse and trifles can be made the day before serving, but the tartlets are best done not too far in advance or the shortbread will go a little soft.

Orange mousse

• 1 tablespoon Cointreau or other orange-flavoured liqueur
• 4 heaped tablespoons orange marmalade • finely grated zest of 1 unwaxed orange
• 1/3 quantity chilled *Crème pâtissière* (roughly 200g, see page 274)
• 150ml double cream, whipped

Mix the liqueur with the marmalade and divide between 4 glasses. Save a little of the orange zest for the decoration, add the rest to the pastry cream and beat until smooth. Fold in half the whipped cream to lighten the mixture and then fold in the rest. Divide the mousse between the glasses, then tap each glass on the work surface to make sure that there are no air pockets. Chill for at least an hour before serving. »»»

Blackcurrant trifles

- 4 sponge fingers • 4 tablespoons *crème de cassis*
- ⅓ quantity chilled *Crème pâtissière* (roughly 200g, see page 274)
- 50g blackcurrants, stalks removed, plus 4 small sprigs for decoration
- sugar (optional) • 100ml double cream, whipped

Break a sponge finger into small pieces and fit them into the bottom of a glass. Repeat with 3 more glasses. Pour 1 tablespoon *crème de cassis* into each glass. Beat the pastry cream until smooth. Crush the blackcurrants a little and mix with the pastry cream. If the blackcurrants are very sour, add a little sugar. Divide the pastry cream between the glasses, then tap each glass on the work surface to make sure that there are no air bubbles. Top with whipped cream. Chill for at least an hour before serving decorated with sprigs of blackcurrants.

Strawberry tartlets

- 4 round shortbread biscuits • 12–15 strawberries
- ⅓ quantity chilled *Crème pâtissière* (roughly 200g, see page 274)

Beat the pastry cream until smooth. Put it into a piping bag fitted with a round 1cm nozzle and pipe a small blob in the middle of each shortbread biscuit (leave some room around the edge for the strawberries). Cut the strawberries in half and stick them around the pastry cream. Serve as soon as you can.

Preparation time: 45 minutes
Resting time: 1 hour (for the pastry cream)
Cooking time: 20 minutes

Les soufflés

Soufflés

Soufflés have a reputation for being difficult, but they really aren't as daunting as you think. A sweet soufflé is simply a meringue mixture folded into pastry cream and baked.

The great thing about this recipe is that you can prepare half of it in advance, leaving you with just some last-minute whisking and folding while the oven is preheating. Pop the soufflés in the oven and 20 minutes later you can impress your guests with a magnificently risen dessert.

- ½ quantity chilled *Crème pâtissière* (roughly 300g, see page 274), with flavouring of your choice

For the ramekins • 4 tablespoons soft butter • 6 tablespoons raw cane sugar*

For the meringue • 60g egg whites (roughly 2 medium egg whites) • 50g icing sugar
• a couple of drops of lemon juice • a pinch of salt

Preheat the oven to 200°C. Brush 4 ramekins with soft butter, working with upward strokes from the bottom to the top. Check that the entire inside of each dish has been covered with butter before adding a heaped tablespoon of raw cane sugar. Roll and tilt each ramekin so that the sugar coats the inside evenly.

To make the meringue, put half the egg whites into a clean glass or metal bowl. Add the sugar, lemon juice and salt and whisk until snow white. Add the rest of the egg whites and continue whisking until the meringue forms stiff peaks.

Beat the pastry cream until smooth and then mix in half the meringue until fully incorporated. Gently fold in the rest of the meringue.

Divide the mix between the ramekins and tap the base of each ramekin on the work surface to ensure there are no air pockets. Level the surface of each soufflé by pulling a palette knife (or back edge of a large knife) across the top of the dish, then clean any drips off the outside or they will burn. To help the soufflés rise, run your thumbnail around the top edge of each ramekin to make a groove.

Put the ramekins into the oven immediately and drop the temperature down to 180°C. Bake for 15–20 minutes or until the soufflés have risen by two-thirds of their original size and wobble a little when moved. Serve straight away.

* *Alternative coatings: mix the sugar with a little ground cinnamon or ginger, or with chilli powder (this works particularly well with a chocolate soufflé), or finely grated citrus zest. The sugar can also be replaced with unsweetened cocoa powder.*

Preparation time: 40 minutes
Resting time: 1 hour (for the pastry cream) Cooking time: 30 minutes

Mousse aux éclats de chocolat

Chocolate mousse with cocoa nibs

This is for any serious chocaholic. A chocolate *crème Madame* (chocolate pastry cream and whipped cream folded together) makes for an easy and delicious chocolate mousse, but I like something with more of a chocolate attitude.

Each element is vital – chocolate pastry cream for a silky-smooth feel, meringue and whipped cream to make it airy and melted dark chocolate to give an extra-rich chocolate flavour. I also like to coat my serving glasses with cocoa nibs to add a bitter chocolate crunch. If you can't get hold of cocoa nibs (available at specialist food shops, online and at some supermarkets), a coating of finely chopped nuts mixed with some cocoa powder is a good alternative.

So this, *Mesdames et Messieurs*, is my ultimate chocolate mousse.

• 2 tablespoons soft butter • 40g cocoa nibs, plus extra for serving
• ½ quantity chilled *Crème pâtissière* (roughly 300g, see page 274), made with 1 tablespoon unsweetened cocoa powder instead of vanilla

For the chocolate meringue • 60g egg whites (roughly 2 medium egg whites)
• 50g icing sugar • a couple of drops of lemon juice • a pinch of salt
• 1 heaped tablespoon unsweetened cocoa powder
• 150g dark chocolate, finely chopped • 200ml whipping cream

Brush 4–6 glasses or ramekins with soft butter. Add some cocoa nibs and roll them around the sides and bottom of the glasses until evenly coated.

To make the meringue, put half the egg whites into a clean glass or metal bowl. Add the sugar, lemon juice and salt and whisk until snow white. Add the rest of the egg whites and continue whisking until the meringue forms stiff peaks.

Melt the chocolate in a *bain marie* (a heatproof bowl set over a pot of simmering water) or in the microwave on a low setting. Whip the cream to soft peaks.

Beat the pastry cream to remove any lumps before stirring in the melted chocolate. Mix in one-third of the meringue, then gently fold in the rest followed by the whipped cream.

Divide the mousse between the glasses and chill for at least an hour. Serve chilled, sprinkled with cocoa nibs. The mousse is best eaten the same day and should not be kept for more than 2 days (due to the raw egg whites).

Preparation time: 45 minutes Resting time: 2 hours
(including the pastry cream) Cooking time: 35 minutes

Millefeuille aux pommes

Apple millefeuille

Don't be put off by the length of this recipe. It's really quite simple, as it uses ready-made puff pastry and everything can be prepared in advance. In fact, the fillings are best made beforehand to give them time to chill in the fridge. All that's left to do before serving is the assembly.

• 250g ready-made puff pastry • 3–4 tablespoons icing sugar • ½ quantity chilled *Crème pâtissière* (roughly 300g, see page 274) • a knob of butter, melted • 4 tablespoons caraway seeds

For the apple compote • 6 dessert apples, peeled and roughly chopped • 1 tablespoon Calvados • 2 tablespoons sugar, or more to taste • 1 leaf of gelatine (2g)*

Cook the apples, Calvados and sugar in a covered pan on a medium heat for 10 minutes or until the apples are soft. Whizz to a smooth purée in a blender, then taste and add more sugar if needed (don't make it too sweet as the pastry cream is quite sweet). Soak the gelatine in cold water for 10 minutes or until soft. Drain and squeeze out the excess water, then dissolve in the warm apple purée. Refrigerate until cold (it will keep in an airtight container in the fridge for up to a week).

Line a large baking tray with baking paper. Dust your rolling pin and work surface with icing sugar. Roll out the pastry to a 30 x 20cm rectangle ½cm thick. Brush with melted butter, dust with icing sugar and sprinkle with caraway seeds. Dust with icing sugar a second time and cut into twelve 10 x 5cm rectangles. Lay the rectangles on the prepared baking tray and place in the fridge. Preheat the oven to 200°C. Bake the pastry for 20 minutes or until golden, then transfer to a wire rack until cold.

To assemble, put the pastry cream and compote into 2 separate piping bags fitted with small plain nozzles. Start by piping 2 blobs of pastry cream on to an individual serving plate and sticking a pastry rectangle on top. Pipe 2 lines of compote on the pastry, then gently place another rectangle over the compote. Pipe 2 lines of pastry cream on the second rectangle and top with a third rectangle. Repeat to make 4 millefeuilles altogether. Serve immediately.

* For a vegetarian version, instead of the gelatine use ½ teaspoon agar agar powder. Add the powder to the apple purée in a pan and boil for 5 minutes, stirring continuously.

Other millefeuille ideas:
• Chocolate *Crème pâtissière* (see page 274). Replace the caraway seeds with chopped hazelnuts.
• Top the pastry cream with fresh berries. Replace the apple compote with another layer of pastry cream and berries.

Preparation time: 1 hour
Resting time: 2 hours (including pastry cream) Cooking time: 1 hour

Pommes rôties au four avec une sauce béchamel sucrée et épicée

Baked apples with sweet spiced béchamel sauce

Paris, as beautiful as it is, has about the same amount of cold, wet and grey days as London, although my Parisian friends would hotly dispute this. On those days, curling up on the couch with a steaming bowl of something sweetly spiced is my remedy for the miserable weather. Both spices and sweetness in this recipe can be adapted to your taste, and the sauce can be kept in the fridge for a day or two, ready to be gently reheated when you want it (whisk in a dash of milk if it's become too thick).

• **6 dessert apples** • **6 cinnamon sticks**

For the sweet béchamel sauce • **30g butter** • **30g plain flour**
• **500ml milk, lukewarm** • **½ vanilla pod, cut widthways** • **4 tablespoons sugar**
• **finely grated zest of ¼ unwaxed orange** • **¼ teaspoon ground ginger**
• **½ teaspoon ground cinnamon** • **a pinch of nutmeg** • **1 clove**

Preheat the oven to 150°C. Core each apple and place a cinammon stick in each core. Wrap each apple tightly in baking paper or aluminium foil and tie with kitchen string. Bake for 15–20 minutes or until the apples are soft but not collapsing.

Meanwhile, make the sauce. Melt the butter in a large pan over a medium heat. Add the flour and beat hard until you have a smooth paste. Take off the heat and leave to cool for 2 minutes, then gradually add the milk, whisking constantly.

Split the vanilla pod in half lengthways and scrape out the grains. Place the pan back over a medium heat and add the pod and grains, the sugar, orange zest and spices. Simmer gently for about 10 minutes, whisking frequently to make sure the sauce doesn't burn on the bottom of the pan. If the sauce becomes too thick, whisk in a little more milk. When the sauce is ready, remove the vanilla pod and clove before pouring the sauce into a jug.

To serve, unwrap the apples and stand them upright on individual plates. Let each person take out their cinnamon stick before pouring a generous helping of sauce over the apple.

Preparation time: 15 minutes   Baking time: 15–20 minutes

Crème brûlée

Caramel-topped custard

On my first trip to Paris I ordered a *crème brûlée* and it tasted awful. In my virtually non-existent French, I tried in vain to complain to the waiter that it tasted burned, only for him to retort that it was *crème brûlée* and meant to be burned. Fortunately now my French is good enough to explain that *crème brûlée* is a rich custard topped with a hard caramel, not a burned caramel.

The classic *crème brûlée* is just cream, egg yolks, sugar and vanilla but I use a combination of cream and milk, which makes a rich custard without the heaviness of using only cream. In summer I often put a small handful of raspberries or blueberries (or a few halved strawberries) into the bottom of each ramekin before completely submerging them in the custard.

• 300ml double cream • 200ml milk • 1 vanilla pod • 6 egg yolks • 100g sugar

For the caramel topping • 30g caster sugar • 30g raw cane sugar

Pour the cream and milk into a pan. Split the vanilla pod in half lengthways and scrape out the grains. Add the pod and grains to the cream and milk. Bring to a boil, turn off the heat and remove the pod from the pan.

Combine the egg yolks with the sugar in a bowl, then slowly pour in the hot cream, whisking continuously. Do not overwhisk as you want to avoid creating too many bubbles.

If you have time, pour the custard into a bowl, cover with cling film and refrigerate overnight. This gives the vanilla grains more time to flavour the cream and milk.

Preheat the oven to 110°C. Divide the custard between 6 wide, shallow ramekins and place in a roasting tin. Pour cold water into the tin to come halfway up the ramekins. Bake for 30–40 minutes or until the custard is set around the edges but still slightly wobbly in the middle. Remove the ramekins from the water and set aside until cooled to room temperature. Cover the ramekins with cling film (don't let it touch the custard), and refrigerate for at least 4 hours, or overnight.

When ready to serve, make the caramel topping. Uncover the ramekins and check to see if condensation has collected on the custards. If it has, gently place paper towels on the surface to soak up the moisture. Mix the two types of sugar together and sprinkle a nice even layer of sugar over each custard. Do this by holding the spoon at least 30cm away from the ramekin – sprinkling from a height is the best way to create an even layer of sugar.   »»»

Place the ramekins on a metal tray. For best results, use a hand-held blowtorch and hold it 10–12cm away from the sugar. Move the flame slowly around the sugar, maintaining a slow and even motion. Stop torching just before the desired degree of caramelization is reached, as the sugar will continue to cook for a few seconds after the flame has been removed.

If you don't have a blowtorch, take a large metal spoon and hold it in a gas flame until very hot (it will turn blue, almost black in colour). Place the spoon on the sugar and move it around so that the heat of the spoon caramelizes the sugar.

Why not try something different instead of vanilla?

The key is to add dry ingredients or just a teaspoon or two of liquid flavouring (e.g. almond extract, orange flower water, rose water) to the cream and milk before bringing to a boil – any more liquid and there's a risk of the custard not setting. Here are some ideas.

- *1 teaspoon dried lavender (strain it out before combining the cream and milk with the egg yolks and sugar).*
- *Finely grated zest of 1 unwaxed orange or lemon.*
- *½ teaspoon ground cinnamon and ¼ teaspoon ground ginger.*
- *½ teaspoon freshly ground black pepper or Indonesian long pepper (this goes particularly well with raspberries in the crème brûlée).*
- *A pinch of saffron threads.*

Tips

- *The custard can be made up to 4 days in advance, but the caramel topping has to be done just before serving. Caramel becomes soft with time, due to the humidity in the air.*
- *You need wide, shallow ramekins to get a high caramel to custard ratio, which is key for a successful crème brûlée.*
- *If you're not using the leftover egg whites straight away, freeze them in an airtight container with the date on the label and use within a month. They can also be kept in the fridge for several days.*

Preparation time: 20 minutes Baking time: 30–40 minutes
Resting time: 4 hours–overnight

Crème caramel

Vanilla cream with caramel sauce

I loved this dessert when I was a kid – French food wasn't very common at home. Growing up in the UK with an Austrian mum and a Malay–Chinese Dad meant that meals were a fusion of Alpine sweetness and south-east Asian spiciness, with a traditional British roast on Sundays. My mum's version of *crème caramel* was courtesy of a powdered mix and it didn't bother me at all. Considering how simple it is to make, nowadays I prefer the real deal.

• 500ml milk • 1 vanilla pod • 60g sugar • 3 eggs plus 2 egg yolks • pouring cream, to serve

For the caramel sauce • 250g sugar

Preheat the oven to 110°C. Sprinkle a thin layer of sugar over the bottom of a heavy-based pan and place on a medium heat. Once the sugar starts to melt, add some more. Repeat several times until all the sugar has melted. Continue heating the caramel, swirling it around in the pan (do not stir).* When the caramel is almost a Coca-Cola colour, add a couple of tablespoons of water (stand back a little as it may splutter). Pour some caramel into a ramekin and immediately swirl it all over the bottom of the dish. Repeat with 5 more ramekins, working very fast as the caramel sets quickly. Set the ramekins aside while you make the cream.

Pour the milk into a pan. Split the vanilla pod lengthways and scrape out the grains. Add the pod and grains to the milk and bring to a boil. Remove from the heat and take out the pod. Combine the eggs and sugar in a bowl, then slowly pour in the hot milk, whisking continuously. Do not overwhisk as you want to avoid creating too many bubbles.

Divide the mixture between the ramekins and place in a roasting tin. Pour cold water into the tin to come halfway up the sides of the ramekins. Bake for 30–40 minutes or until the cream is set around the edges but still slightly wobbly in the middle. Remove the ramekins from the water and set aside until cooled to room temperature. Cover with cling film (don't let it touch the custard), and refrigerate for at least 4 hours, or overnight.

To serve, run a knife around the top edge of the cream and dip each ramekin in boiling water for about 30 seconds. Invert a plate on top of the ramekin, then turn both over and give them a shake or two to release the vanilla cream and caramel sauce on to the plate. Serve chilled, with a jug of pouring cream.

* **Pourquoi?** *Using a spoon to stir the caramel will agitate the sugar molecules and make the caramel crystallize.*

Preparation time: 20 minutes Baking time: 30–40 minutes
Resting time: 4 hours–overnight

Iles flottantes

Floating islands

Iles flottantes are the perfect finish to any rich meal. Egg whites are whisked into the lightest meringue and gently poached, then floated on a lake of creamy, cold *crème anglaise* and topped with praline.

Crème anglaise is one of the all-time classic French dessert sauces, and a great one to have under your belt. Once you understand the technique, you'll be able to adapt the recipe with your own flavourings. I like to add some freshly ground long pepper, which is sweet and spicy and gives the whole thing a little kick. (You're most likely to find long pepper at an Asian supermarket, or it can be replaced with regular black pepper.)

This dessert should be served cold, which makes it perfect for preparing in advance. The praline can be made a couple of weeks before you need it and the *crème anglaise* a couple of days ahead. Keep the praline in an airtight container, as humidity will make it soggy and sticky. The meringues are best made on the day of serving.

For the crème anglaise • 4 egg yolks • 80g sugar • 1 vanilla pod • 500ml milk
• ½ teaspoon ground long pepper or black pepper (optional)

For the praline • 75g sugar • 25ml water • 50g slivered almonds

For the islands • 2 egg whites (60g) • 45g icing sugar, sifted if lumpy
• a couple of drops of lemon juice • a pinch of salt

To make the *crème anglaise*, mix the egg yolks and sugar together in a bowl. Split the vanilla pod in half lengthways and scrape out the grains. Place the pod and grains in a pan with the milk and pepper and bring to a boil. Remove the pod, then pour a little of the hot milk onto the egg yolks and sugar, whisking continuously. Gradually whisk in the rest of the milk, then pour the mix into a clean pan, set over a gentle heat and whisk constantly. Do not let the custard simmer at any point or it will split. After 5 minutes it will begin to thicken slightly and become the consistency of single cream (it will thicken more when it cools down). Transfer to a bowl and chill in the fridge for at least 4 hours.

Meanwhile, make the praline. Line a baking tray with baking paper. Put the sugar and water into a large pan, heat gently until the sugar dissolves, then increase the heat to high. When the mixture starts to bubble, add the almonds and stir continuously for 5 minutes to prevent them from sticking to the bottom of the pan and burning. Once the sugar and nuts have become a dark golden caramel colour, pour on to the prepared tray and spread as thinly as possible with a palette knife (be quick as it sets pretty fast). Leave to cool.

»»»

To make the islands, put half the egg whites into a clean glass or metal bowl. Add the sugar, lemon juice and salt and whisk until snow white. Add the rest of the egg whites and continue whisking until the meringue forms stiff peaks.

Gently drop 6 spoonfuls of meringue into a large pot of simmering water* and simmer for a few minutes or until they are slightly puffed up and just set. Remove with a slotted spoon and place on a sheet of baking paper until needed.

To assemble, pour a ladleful of *crème anglaise* into each of 6 glasses and gently place a meringue in the centre. Snap the praline into small pieces and sprinkle on top.

* *If you prefer you can cook the islands in the microwave. Spoon 6 small heaps onto a plate, leaving at least 2cm between each one, and microwave on medium-high for 30–60 seconds.*

The vanilla pod can be interchanged with different flavourings. Here are a few ideas to get your imagination going.

Winter warming: *1 cinnamon stick, ½ teaspoon ground ginger and a pinch of nutmeg.*
Chocolate chilli: *4 tablespoons unsweetened cocoa powder and 2 pinches of chilli powder, or to taste.*
Zingy citrus fruit: *finely grated zest of 1 unwaxed orange, ½ lemon and ½ lime.*

Preparation time: 45 minutes   Resting time: 4 hours
Cooking time: 30 minutes

Mont blanc

Meringue and chestnut-cream mountain

With only three main ingredients – meringue, whipped cream and sweetened chestnut cream – there's really not much to this dessert. And if you're short of time, you could even get away with buying the ingredients ready-made and just assembling them before serving.

Traditionally the chestnut cream should be thick enough to be piped, but I like mine a little runnier, so that I can pour it over the meringues and cream to make them look like mini mountains – hence the name Mont Blanc.

For the meringues • 90g egg whites (roughly 3 medium egg whites) • 75g icing sugar
• a couple of drops of lemon juice • a pinch of salt

For the chestnut cream • 1 vanilla pod • 200g cooked chestnuts (from a jar or tin is fine)
• 250ml double cream • 30g golden caster sugar • 1½ tablespoons Cognac (optional)

To assemble • 200ml whipping cream

To make the meringues, preheat the oven to 80°C and line a baking tray with baking paper. Put half the egg whites into a clean glass or metal bowl. Add the sugar, lemon juice and salt and whisk until snow white. Add the rest of the egg whites and continue whisking until the meringue forms stiff peaks.

Spoon 4 heaped peaks of meringue onto the prepared tray (ideally they should look like mini mountains). Bake for 2 hours or until crisp, opening the oven door a few times to release any steam. Remove them from the paper and leave to cool on a wire rack. (Once cold, the meringues can be kept in an airtight container for a good couple of days.)

To make the chestnut cream, split the vanilla pod in half lengthways and scrape out the grains. Put the pod and grains into a pot with the rest of the ingredients and bring to a simmer on a medium heat. Simmer for 10 minutes or until the chestnuts are soft and slightly mushy. Remove the vanilla pod and whizz the chestnuts to a soft, creamy purée in an electric blender. Chill until needed (it will keep for up to a week in an airtight container).

To assemble, whip the cream to soft peaks. Place the meringues on individual plates, spoon over the whipped cream and pour over the chestnut cream (if it has set too thick, whisk in some double cream). Serve straight away.

Preparation time: 30 minutes Resting time: 1 hour
Baking time: 2 hours

Vacherin 'hotdog' avec rhubarbe au romarin

Vacherin 'hotdog' with rosemary rhubarb

A *vacherin* dessert is not to be confused with the gooey, pungent cheese of the same name. Apart from the name and shape, they have little else in common. The dessert is composed of large meringue discs layered with whipped cream and fruit. It looks stunning until you try and cut it, when it turns into meringue-and-cream carnage. I find it easier to make individual portions, and I also think it's fun to pipe the meringues and sandwich them together with rhubarb and cream to resemble hotdogs.

For the compote • 2–3 stalks of rhubarb • 80g golden caster sugar • 1 sprig of rosemary

For the meringue • 60g egg whites (roughly 2 medium egg whites)
• 50g icing sugar • a pinch of salt • a couple of drops of lemon juice

To assemble • 200ml whipping cream

Trim the rhubarb and cut the stalks into 8 pieces, each about 10cm long. Put the sugar and rosemary into a pan over a medium heat and heat until the sugar has melted. Add the rhubarb and turn the heat down to low, then cover and cook gently for 5–10 minutes or until the rhubarb is tender but still holds its shape. Leave to cool, then remove the rosemary. (The rhubarb tastes better if it's cooked at least a day in advance and it can be kept in the fridge for up to a week.)

To make the meringue, preheat the oven to 80°C and line a baking tray with baking paper. Put half the egg whites into a clean glass or metal bowl. Add the sugar, lemon juice and salt and whisk until snow white. Add the rest of the egg whites and continue whisking until the meringue forms stiff peaks.

Spoon the meringue into a piping bag fitted with a 1cm nozzle and pipe eight 10cm-long strips onto the prepared tray. Bake for 2 hours or until crisp, opening the oven door a few times to release any steam. Remove the meringues from the paper and leave to cool on a wire rack. (Once cold, they can be kept in an airtight container for a good couple of days.)

To assemble, whip the cream to stiff peaks and spoon into a piping bag fitted with a 5mm nozzle. Lift the rhubarb out of its juice and drain well. Pipe a line of cream on the flat side of 2 pieces of meringue and sandwich 2 pieces of rhubarb between them. Repeat to make 4 hotdogs altogether and serve straight away.

Preparation time: 30–45 minutes Baking time: 2 hours

Tartelettes aux framboises et amandes

Raspberry and almond tartlets

When I tell French people that I studied and now teach *pâtisserie*, their eyes often light up. One friend was so impressed with these tartlets that he nicknamed me '*Tartelette*'. Translated as 'little tart', this may sound rather dubious, but in French it doesn't have the same connotation.

• 90g soft butter • 1 teaspoon sugar • a pinch of salt
• 180g plain flour • 2 egg yolks • 2 tablespoons ice-cold water

For the almond cream • 200g ground almonds • 200g sugar
• 200g soft butter • 2 eggs • 300g raspberries*

Make the pastry. Using a wooden spoon, beat together the butter, sugar and salt until soft and creamy. Mix in the flour followed by the egg yolks and 2 tablespoons ice-cold water. Bring together to make a smooth ball, adding a little more water if the pastry is too crumbly (only knead as much as necessary to bring the dough together). Wrap the dough in cling film and refrigerate for a minimum of an hour (best overnight).

Beat the almonds, sugar and butter just until smooth, then beat in the eggs.

Remove the pastry from the fridge 30 minutes before using and preheat the oven to 180°C. Roll out the pastry between 2 sheets of baking paper until 3–5mm thick. Cut out 4 rectangles of pastry large enough to line four 11.5 x 6.5cm tartlet tins with a 2cm overhang. Place the pastry in the tins and prick each base several times with a fork. Spread the almond cream in the pastry cases and arrange the raspberries on top, keeping them close together so that they almost cover the cream. Trim off the pastry overhang.

Bake for 15–20 minutes or until the pastry edges are golden brown. Best eaten warm. Cold is fine too (but not refrigerated).

* *Any kind of fruit works, even tinned and frozen (thawed), as long as it's drained of excess liquid.*

** *If you prefer, you can make 6 round tartlets in 10cm tartlet tins, or 1 large 23cm tart. The baking time for the large tart will be 30 minutes.*

Preparation time: 20 minutes Resting time: 1 hour–overnight
Baking time: 15–20 minutes

Tarte Tatin

Upside-down apple tart

In the late nineteenth century the Tatin sisters came up with this great recipe at their restaurant in Lamotte-Beuvron in the Sologne. It was all an accident, apparently. They burned their apple tart and decided to remove the burned pastry at the bottom, keep the caramelized apples and put new pastry on the top. Who said that accidents can't be a good thing in the kitchen?

My version has the pastry baked separately instead of over the apples. This way, the pastry stays crisp rather than going soggy.

The traditional *tarte Tatin* calls for a classic caramel sauce but I like to make a salted caramel sauce, which is typically Breton.

• 250g puff pastry • 14–16 dessert apples • a knob of butter, melted • sugar, for sprinkling

For the salted caramel • 100g sugar • 2 knobs of soft butter • 1 teaspoon salt

Preheat the oven to 180°C. Roll out the pastry on a floured surface until it is 1cm thick and cut out a disc that is a couple of millimetres bigger than a 25cm round tart tin. Place the pastry on a baking tray and prick all over with a fork. Bake for 30 minutes or until the pastry is puffy and golden.

Meanwhile, make the salted caramel. Sprinkle a thin layer of sugar over the bottom of a heavy-based pan and place on a medium heat. Once the sugar starts to melt, add some more sugar. Repeat a couple of times until all the sugar has melted. Continue heating the caramel, swirling it around in the pan (do not stir). When the caramel is almost a Coca-Cola colour, take the pan off the heat and swirl in the butter (stand back a little as it may splutter) and add the salt. Pour the caramel into the tart tin and swirl it around to cover the bottom and sides.

Peel, core and halve the apples. Sit them tightly upright in the tart tin, making sure they are really snug (they shrink when they cook). You can cut the last apple into quarters to stuff some of the large holes. Brush the apples with the melted butter and sprinkle some sugar on top. Bake for 30 minutes or until the apples are tender but not mushy. Remove from the oven and leave the apples to cool until they are not too hot to the touch.

To assemble, place the pastry on top of the apples, then invert a large dinner plate on top of the pastry. Turn the tart and the plate over so that the apples come out on top of the pastry. Serve straight away, with ice cream or a dollop of *crème fraîche*.

Preparation time: 30 minutes Baking time: 1 hour
Resting time: 30 minutes

Moelleux au chocolat

Chocolate lava cake

Cook'n with Class is a little cookery school in Montmartre where I used to teach French *pâtisserie*. The students are a pretty international crowd, from young backpackers and honeymooners to pensioners, but they all have a few classic dessert recipes that they would like to learn. One of the top-ten favourites is *moelleux au chocolat*.

Moelleux means soft or tender, which perfectly describes this dessert. Like a volcano, the cake has a centre that explodes when you dive in with your spoon.

Special thanks for this recipe to Eric Fraudeau, the owner at Cook'n with Class.

• 170g dark chocolate, finely chopped • 170g butter, cubed • 170g light brown sugar
• 85g plain flour • 6 eggs, beaten

For the ramekins • 30g soft butter • 30g unsweetened cocoa powder

Prepare 6–8 ramekins by brushing them with the butter and then dusting with the cocoa powder. Make sure to tap out all the excess cocoa powder.

Melt the chocolate with the butter in a *bain marie* (a heatproof bowl set over a pan of simmering water), stirring occasionally. Alternatively, melt them in the microwave on a low setting.

Combine the sugar and flour in a bowl. Mix the melted chocolate with the eggs followed by the flour and sugar. Divide the mixture between the ramekins and refrigerate for a minimum of 1 hour.*

Preheat the oven to 180°C. Bake the cakes for 15–20 minutes or until the edges are firm and the centres slightly runny. Test by inserting a toothpick in the centre – it should come out wet. Leave to rest for 2 minutes before turning the cakes out of the ramekins on to plates. Serve immediately, with vanilla ice cream, whipped cream or fresh berries.

* *Pourquoi? Baking your batter from cold will make it slower for the heat from the oven to penetrate the middle of the cakes, which will make the centres all the more gooey. The ramekins filled with the batter can be covered with cling film (don't let it touch the batter) and kept in the fridge for several days. They can also be well wrapped in cling film and frozen, then baked from frozen (they will need an extra 5–10 minutes in the oven – test to see if they are done as above).*

Preparation time: 20 minutes Resting time: 1 hour
Baking time: 15–20 minutes

Moelleux au chocolat coeur fondant caramel salé

Chocolate lava cake with salted caramel filling

At Cook'n with Class they tend to keep *moelleux au chocolat* simple and serve it just as it comes, but when I'm at home I like to pipe a little salted caramel filling into the centre, which makes it even harder to say *non* to this dessert. The salted caramel recipe makes a little more than you need for the *moelleux au chocolat,* but it's good with virtually anything – on toast, ice cream, stirred into plain yoghurt…

• *Moelleux au chocolat* (see left)

For the salted caramel filling • 150g sugar • 150ml double cream
• 1 teaspoon *fleur de sel* or coarse sea salt

Follow the recipe opposite for *moelleux au chocolat,* but only fill the ramekins three-quarters full with the chocolate mixture.

To make the caramel, sprinkle a thin layer of sugar over the bottom of a heavy-based pan and place on a medium heat. Once the sugar starts to melt, add some more sugar. Repeat a couple of times until all the sugar has melted. Continue heating the caramel, swirling it around in the pan (do not stir).* When the caramel is almost a Coca-Cola colour, add the cream and salt (be careful as the caramel may splutter). Cook until the temperature reaches 108°C, or until the caramel coats the back of a spoon, then pour into a dish and leave to cool a little.

Once the caramel is cool, transfer it to a piping bag fitted with a small round nozzle, or to a heavy-duty food bag (just snip off the corner to use). Pop the piping nozzle into the middle of the chocolate mixture in each ramekin and squirt in the filling (the mixture will rise almost to the top).

Bake and serve as for *moelleux au chocolat.*

For an alternative fruit filling, warm 200g jam (raspberry, orange, mango…) in a pan or in the microwave until runny, then whizz in an electric blender until smooth. Leave to cool before piping into the ramekins as for the salted caramel filling.

* *Pourquoi? Using a spoon to stir the caramel will agitate the sugar molecules and make the caramel crystallize.*

Preparation time: 30 minutes Resting time: 1 hour
Baking time: 15–20 minutes

Sabayon de Champagne avec fraises gariguettes et tomates cerises

Champagne sabayon with strawberries and cherry tomatoes

According to scientists, strawberries and tomatoes should be interchangeable in recipes as they share the same flavour components, and I think my little scientific experiment has turned out pretty well, adding a modern twist to this classic recipe.

Like the English, the French love their strawberries, and one of the most popular varieties is the *gariguette*. Elongated and conical in shape, with a delicate sweet flavour, *gariguettes* are delicious eaten on their own or in this light and fluffy dish.

- 200g strawberries (*gariguettes* if you can get them), halved or quartered
- 100g cherry tomatoes, quartered and deseeded

For the sabayon • 4 egg yolks • 25g sugar • 100ml Champagne

To make the sabayon, put the egg yolks and sugar into a *bain marie* (a heatproof bowl set over a pan of simmering water) and whisk until pale yellow and thick. Add the Champagne and continue whisking until the sabayon is very thick and foamy, about 10 minutes. To test, draw a figure of eight in the mixture with the whisk – if the figure stays put, then the sabayon is ready.

Divide the sabayon between 4 bowls, place the strawberries and tomatoes on top and serve straight away. Alternatively, chill the sabayon until ready to use (a couple of hours is fine) and add the strawberries and tomatoes just before serving.

Preparation time: 10 minutes Cooking time: 10–15 minutes

Poires Belle Hélène

Beautiful Helen pears

In the late nineteenth century, Auguste Escoffier found inspiration for this recipe in Offenbach's operetta *La Belle Hélène*. The beauty of the dish lies in its simplicity: pears poached in a sugar syrup, served cold with a warm chocolate sauce. I've added cardamom to the chocolate sauce, which gives a lovely warmth.

• 1.5 litres cold water • 1 vanilla pod • 150g sugar
• 4 firm pears (e.g. William), peeled with stalks still attached

For the cardamom chocolate sauce • 100g dark or white chocolate, finely chopped
• 100ml double cream • 3 cardamom pods, crushed

Pour the water into a large pan. Split the vanilla pod in half lengthways and scrape out the grains. Add the pod and grains to the water with the sugar and bring to a simmer, stirring occasionally to dissolve the sugar. Add the pears and place a piece of baking paper on top to keep them submerged, then simmer gently for 20 minutes. Insert a skewer or small sharp knife to test whether the pears are tender. If not, simmer for a further 5 minutes. When the pears are cooked, leave them to cool in the syrup for at least a couple of hours, preferably overnight, to give them time to take on the flavour of the vanilla. (They can be kept in an airtight container in the fridge for a couple of days.)

To make the sauce, put the chocolate into a bowl. Bring the cream to a boil with the crushed cardamom pods and pour over the chocolate. Leave to stand for a minute until the chocolate has melted, remove the cardamom pods (leaving the seeds behind in the sauce), then stir the sauce gently until smooth. Do not overmix or the *ganache* may split – the cocoa solids will separate from the cocoa butter. (The sauce can be made in advance and reheated very gently in the microwave or a *bain marie*.)

To serve, remove the pears from the syrup* and stand them upright on individual plates. Pour a generous helping of chocolate sauce over them and serve with a scoop of vanilla ice cream or a dollop of whipped cream.

* Keep the sugar syrup in the fridge and use for fruit salads.

Preparation time: 20 minutes Resting time: 2 hours–overnight
Cooking time: 30 minutes

Fontainebleau avec un coulis de carotte et cannelle

Fontainebleau with a carrot cinnamon coulis

Unlike the *château* of the same name, the dessert *fontainebleau* is not elaborate. Whipped cream, fromage blanc, sugar and vanilla are simply mixed together and pressed. It makes for a wonderful light ending to a meal and is especially refreshing when served with a cold fruit sauce or a handful of berries – or in this case, with a carrot and cinnamon coulis.

• ½ vanilla pod, cut widthways • 200ml whipping cream • 1 teaspoon sugar
• 200g *fromage blanc* or Quark • ground cinnamon, to serve

For the coulis • 3 carrots, grated • 150ml carrot juice • juice of 1 orange
• 1 tablespoon sugar • a pinch of ground cinnamon

Split the vanilla pod in half lengthways and scrape out the grains. Put the grains into a bowl with the cream and sugar and whisk to stiff peaks. Fold the cream into the *fromage blanc*.

Line a large colander with a clean tea towel and stand the colander in a large bowl. Put the cream mix into the colander and enclose in the tea towel, tying the ends together tightly to make a parcel. Place a heavy pot (you can add water to make it heavier) on top of the tea towel and refrigerate overnight or up to 24 hours.

To make the coulis, put all the ingredients into a pot, cover and bring to a simmer. Cook for 10 minutes and then whizz to a smooth purée in an electric blender. Chill in the fridge until serving time.

To serve, pour the chilled coulis into 4–6 bowls, add a generous scoop of *fontainebleau* to each bowl and sprinkle with a pinch of cinnamon.

Preparation time: 30 minutes Resting time: overnight–24 hours
Cooking time: 10 minutes

Riz rouge au lait d'amande

Red rice pudding with almond milk

There is something creamy and comforting about *riz au lait* that brings back childhood memories for most French people. It's traditionally made with short-grain white rice, milk and cream, but I also like it with red rice from the Camargue (in the south of France). This gives the pudding a fabulous colour as well as a subtle nuttiness, which is accentuated by the almond milk. I'm not shy of piling on a few more calories, so I serve it with *crème Chantilly*.

• 160g red rice • 500ml unsweetened almond milk* • ½ teaspoon almond extract
• 2 tablespoons sugar, or to taste

For the crème Chantilly • ½ vanilla pod, cut widthways
• 150ml whipping cream • 4 tablespoons sugar

Put the rice, almond milk and almond extract into a large pan and bring to a gentle simmer. Cover and simmer gently for 25–30 minutes or until the rice is tender but still slightly nutty in texture. Stir occasionally to make sure the rice doesn't stick to the bottom of the pan.

Meanwhile, make the *crème Chantilly*: split the vanilla pod in half lengthways and scrape out the grains. Put the grains in a bowl with the cream and sugar and whisk to stiff peaks.

Add sugar to taste to the rice and serve the pudding either warm or chilled,** topped with the *crème Chantilly*.

*You can buy almond milk at some large supermarkets, health food shops and online.

** Once cool, chill the rice in a covered container in the fridge for about 4 hours (it will keep for a couple of days). You may need to add a little more almond milk to loosen up the rice before serving.

Preparation time: 5 minutes Cooking time: 30 minutes

Tartelettes au pamplemousse et poivre meringuées

Grapefruit and pepper meringue tartlets

Unlike the *tartelettes* on page 245, these use a traditional Breton biscuit recipe for the base. It's a great alternative to classic pastry as there's no need to chill or roll out the dough. I like to add some freshly ground black pepper to my meringue. It may sound odd, but the little spicy kick works really well with the acidity of the grapefruit curd.

For the grapefruit curd • 1 unwaxed grapefruit • 100g sugar • a pinch of salt • 1 egg plus 1 egg yolk • 1 heaped tablespoon cornflour • 50g soft butter, cubed

For the biscuit base • 75g butter, very soft but not melted • 75g sugar • a generous pinch of salt • finely grated zest of ½ unwaxed lemon • 2 egg yolks • 100g plain flour • 2 teaspoons baking powder

For the Italian meringue* • 100g sugar • 40ml water • 2 egg whites (roughly 60g) • a pinch of salt • ½ teaspoon pepper

* Pourquoi? In French pâtisserie there are three types of meringue:

French – The best-known meringue, for which egg whites are simply whisked with sugar. It is also the least stable as the egg whites are not cooked while being whisked. Best baked immediately or the egg whites begin to deflate. Used in desserts like *vacherin* and *Mont Blanc*, and eaten on their own (like the ones you see in *pâtisserie* windows).

Swiss – Egg whites are whisked with sugar over a *bain marie*, then taken off and whisked until cool and stiff. This technique ensures that the sugar is completely dissolved and makes a very firm meringue. Used for icing and baked decorations (piped into different shapes such as mushrooms or flowers).

Italian – Egg whites are whisked while a hot sugar syrup is poured onto them. This cooks the egg whites, making a stable and stiff meringue. Used for topping cakes, desserts and for making macarons. It is best made using a standalone mixer or a powerful electric hand-held beater.　⟫⟫

To make the grapefruit curd, finely grate the zest of the grapefruit and squeeze the juice. Measure 90ml juice into a pan and whisk together with the zest, sugar, salt and eggs over a gentle heat. Sift in the cornflour and continue to whisk. Don't stop whisking at any point, otherwise the eggs will curdle. Once the curd is as thick as puréed tomatoes and has released a bubble or two, take it off the heat and whisk in the butter a cube at a time. Pour into a bowl and place cling film in direct contact with the curd. Refrigerate for at least an hour (best overnight).

To make the biscuit base,* preheat the oven to 180°C and butter six 8 x 5cm metal dessert rings.** Cream together the butter and sugar with the salt and lemon zest until fluffy and pale in colour. Add the egg yolks and continue to beat. Sift the flour and baking powder together, add to the creamed mixture and continue beating until the dough comes together as a smooth paste. Put the dough into a piping bag fitted with a 1cm round nozzle.

Pipe the dough into the rings to come about 3–4mm high, then use a spoon dipped in hot water to level out the pastry. Bake for 12–15 minutes or until golden (but not too dark). Leave to cool for a couple of minutes before running a small sharp knife around the inside of each ring to release the biscuit. Transfer the biscuits to a wire rack (be careful as they're fragile) and leave to cool.

To make the Italian meringue, put the sugar into a pan with the water and place on a high heat. Bring to the soft-ball stage (118°C on a sugar thermometer), which will take about 10 minutes. To test without a thermometer, drop a tiny bit of sugar syrup into a bowl of very cold water. When it forms a soft sticky ball, it is ready.

While waiting for the sugar syrup, start whisking the egg whites with the salt and pepper in a glass or metal bowl. Do not whisk to soft peaks, just a light froth. Once the sugar syrup has reached the soft-ball stage, beat the egg whites on high speed at the same time as pouring the syrup onto them in a thin stream. (Don't pour the syrup over the whisk, but down the side of the bowl.) Continue to whisk for 10 minutes or until the egg whites are glossy and stiff.

To assemble, spread the grapefruit curd on top of the biscuits followed by the meringue. Either place under a very hot grill for a couple of minutes or use a blowtorch to brown.

* The bases can be eaten on their own as Breton biscuits. They will keep in an airtight container for up to a week.

** Instead of 6 tartelettes you can make 1 large tart in a 25cm tart tin. The baking time will be 30–40 minutes.

Preparation time: 1 hour Resting time: 1 hour–overnight
Cooking time: 30 minutes

Sélection de fromage avec une confiture de tomates cerises et vanille

Cheese selection with cherry tomato and vanilla jam

For me, cheese, wine and a crusty *baguette* are the perfect *ménage à trois*. But which cheese? There are more than two hundred different French cheeses to choose from and it's no wonder that Charles de Gaulle said, 'How can anyone govern a nation that has 246 different kinds of cheese?'

It can be quite daunting to know what to choose, but nowadays there are no set rules. You can get away with just serving one excellent cheese rather than three mediocre ones.

In France many cheeses have the AOC (*appellation d'origine contrôlée)* label. This means that the product's origin is protected and strict guidelines are enforced. (Probably the most commonly known AOC is that of Champagne – sparkling wine produced in the Champagne region is the only one to be allowed the name.)

If you are serving more than one cheese, it's best to start with the mildest so that its flavour is not overpowered by a stronger cheese – i.e. on a cheeseboard, a mild goat's cheese would be the first to eat and a blue cheese the last.

There's an art to everything in France and this applies to cutting cheese as much as anything else. Without getting too technical, a general rule of thumb is that every portion of cheese should include some of the rind (the flavour gets stronger closer to the rind).

When trying to match wine with cheese, it can help to choose a wine produced in the same region as the cheese, e.g. a glass of Calvados (apple liqueur) is a good match with Camembert as they both come from Normandy.

As a general guideline, go by the texture and taste of the cheese rather than the smell. A soft and creamy cheese is equally good with a sweet, soft wine as it is with a tangy acidic wine, whereas strong or salty cheeses normally go best with an acidic wine. Remember, the more mature and salty the cheese, the more aggressive the taste when it is eaten with wine.

The wines listed with the cheeses on page 264 are only suggestions, so don't feel that they are the only ones you can drink with that cheese. At the end of the day, it's all a matter of personal taste.

It's impossible to mention every French cheese, so I've just listed some of the classics that I like and that are easy to find. Should you be lucky enough to have a local *fromagerie*, do try out some of the cheeses that are less well known. »»

Selles-sur-Cher

A goat's cheese that is covered with a layer of charcoal. The rind is meant to be eaten and contributes to the overall flavour, which is slightly acidic and salty with a melt-in-the-mouth mildness. It has a delicate hazelnut aftertaste.

Wine: Sancerre, Pouilly Fumé

Crottin de Chavignol

This goat's cheese is best eaten after it has matured for a minimum of 2 weeks, when it gets a fine layer of blue and white mould and loses some of its moisture. (Otherwise, according to the French, it's not a real *crottin*.) The older it gets, the more crumbly, hard and salty it becomes. When slightly warmed, it is delicious with a simple green salad.

Wine: Sancerre

Brie de Meaux

Produced about 50km east of Paris, this cow's milk cheese is a popular choice on Parisian cheeseboards. It has a light, straw-coloured and velvety soft rind and is slightly creamier and milder than its Normandy cousin, Camembert. There's also *brie noir* that is matured for up to a year, making it a lot denser and drier than the regular *brie*, which is usually matured for 4–6 weeks. The traditional way of eating *brie noir* is to dip it into your coffee at breakfast.

Wine: Saint-Julien, Champagne

Comté

What Cheddar is for the English, Comté is for the French – probably the most popular hard cheese. The best Comté is sold according to its maturing age of 12 months, 18 months or 36 months. The 36 months version often develops salt crystals and has a similar strength to Parmesan. Comté is a cheese that can be used for most things, from sandwiches and soufflés to gratins.

Wine: Côtes du Jura

Morbier

This cow's milk cheese has a thin blue line running through the middle. It was developed by farmers who had morning milk left over from making Comté and sprinkled it with a layer of ash to protect it. The leftover evening milk was then poured on top, and during the maturing process the charcoal developed into a blue mould, giving the cheese its characteristic look and taste.

Wine: Crépy (Savoie)

Camembert

The little village of Camembert in Normandy gives this famous, quite pungent, soft cheese its name. The cheese is ripe when it is soft to touch (it shouldn't be firm), has a creamy yellow colour and a light 'mouldy' smell. There are some Camembert varieties that have their rinds brushed with cider or Calvados.

Wine: Saint-Emilion or Calvados

Roquefort

After Comté, Roquefort comes in second as the most popular cheese for the French. In 1411 the French king Charles VI gave it the AOC label, ensuring that the inhabitants of the village of Roquefort could be the only producers of the famous blue cheese. Roquefort can be extremely strong (eat it last if it is on a cheeseboard with other cheeses), which means a little goes a long way. Due to the slight aggressiveness of the cheese, it is best matched with a sweet wine or one without acidic notes.

Wine: Sauternes

Compotée de tomates cerises et vanille

Cherry tomato and vanilla compote

Marie is the only French friend I know who makes her own jam, sourdough bread and yoghurt. So what better person to ask for a little something to go with cheese? She recommends eating this compote with an aged goat's cheese like *crottin de Chavignol* or a fresh goat's cheese.

• 500g cherry tomatoes of various shapes • a generous pinch of salt
• 3 tablespoons granulated sugar • 3 tablespoons light olive oil • 1 vanilla pod

Wash and dry the tomatoes and cut them in half. Arrange skin-side down on a large non-stick baking tray and sprinkle with the salt and sugar. Set aside at room temperature while you get on with the vanilla oil.

Put the olive oil into a small bowl. Cut the vanilla pod in half lengthways and scrape out the grains. Using a teaspoon, mix the grains with the olive oil. Add the vanilla pod and infuse for 15 minutes.

Preheat the oven to 120°C.

Pour the infused oil (plus the vanilla pod) over the tomatoes and slow roast for 50–60 minutes, checking regularly. Once cooked, the tomatoes will still be red, but some will be very slightly brown.

Serve lukewarm or cold. (The compote will keep for a couple of days in the fridge. Once cool, transfer to a glass jar, scraping the tray for extra caramel, and cover with a tight-fitting lid.)

Preparation time: 20 minutes Resting time: 15 minutes
Cooking time: 50–60 minutes

French Basics

Les bases de la cuisine française

Back to basics

French cuisine is littered with terms, techniques and '*toques*' (the tall white chefs' hats). It may seem all a little old-fashioned and stuffy compared to the laid-back style of the Italians or the molecular madness of the Spanish, but the French still have a lot to say in the kitchen. It's not for no reason that most culinary schools' curricula cover French cuisine. It provides students with a great foundation and understanding of cooking.

French cooking has become so embedded into the Western way of cooking that often we don't realize what we're whipping up has French origins. Take away the foreign language and what you're left with are some fundamental cooking methods. Once you understand these techniques, they can be applied and adapted to a whole variety of dishes, opening up a world of culinary possibilities.

Regardless of whether you're a beginner or a *Masterchef* contestant, knowing a few French culinary a–b–c's such as how to make a basic stock, *béchamel* or salad vinaigrette will help you out in any kitchen situation.

Les Fonds/ Stocks

A liquid in which meat, fish or vegetables are simmered to extract their flavour; used as a base for soups, sauces and stews.

The French word for stock is *fond*. It also means base or foundation, which is a great way of describing how important stocks are in French cuisine. In fact, it's not only French dishes that benefit from a good-quality stock – the value of any dish containing stock will go up if the stock is made well.

You may think that in today's hectic world there's no time to make stock, but it doesn't take as long as you think. Ten minutes' prep and the rest is just letting it simmer gently on the stove. You'll be rewarded with something that has so much more depth and flavour than the little cubes you dissolve in water (and none of the additives).

Water, the main component of stock, costs next to nothing. You need to add your key ingredient – meat or fish bones or vegetables – plus what the French call *mirepoix* (onion, carrot and celery) and a bouquet garni. A classic bouquet garni would be a bay leaf, peppercorns, parsley stalks and thyme.

So, the ingredients stay practically the same regardless of what kind of stock you're making, and so does the technique. Simply pop the ingredients into a pot, simmer and skim off the scum (the impurities and fat that rise to the surface).

There are two different types of stock in French cuisine: white (unroasted) and brown (roasted). White stock is generally used for white sauces due to its colour, while brown stock has a stronger colour and flavour.

Each stock uses a key component that gives it a distinct flavour:

Veal/beef
Knuckles are best as they contain collagen, which gives the stock body. The French prefer veal to beef because it makes a lighter and more delicately flavoured stock (it also contains more collagen).

Poultry
Carcasses, backs and wings of chicken or turkey (or the bird of your preference).

Fish/shellfish
Bones and heads of white fish (e.g. pollack, haddock, sole). Avoid oily fish, such as mackerel, tuna or salmon, as they will make a cloudy stock. Shells from crustaceans (e.g. prawns, crabs, langoustines, lobsters) also make a flavoursome stock.

Vegetable
Aromatic vegetables, such as leeks, fennel, parsnips and celery. Mushrooms lend a meaty flavour. Avoid potatoes, sweet potatoes, pumpkins and other starchy vegetables as they will make a cloudy stock.

Tips for a successful stock
- The golden rule for making a meat or fish stock is to start with cold water, bring it slowly to a simmer, and then keep it on a simmer throughout the cooking time.

Pourquoi? A cold start and slow heating release water-soluble proteins, which coagulate slowly into the stock and rise to the top, making it easier to skim. (A hot start produces many separate and tiny protein particles that create a murky stock, while a rolling boil makes the fat and scum come to the top and then emulsify back into the stock.)

- For all meat and fish stocks, use a combination of bones and meat with no fat.

Pourquoi? When you simmer bones, the collagen turns into gelatine and is absorbed into the stock to give it body and a silky mouth feel. Bones don't provide much flavour, however, so that's where the meat comes into play, giving the stock taste.

Storage
Fresh meat, poultry and vegetable stocks can be kept in an airtight container in the fridge for up to 5 days, or in the freezer for up to 3 months. Fish stock is best used the same day.

To save on storage space, simmer the stock until reduced by half and then pour into ice-cube trays and freeze. Whenever you need stock for a recipe, use a frozen cube of your own home-made stock.

WHITE (UNROASTED) STOCK
MAKES ABOUT I LITRE

- 1.5kg raw veal or beef knuckles/poultry carcasses, backs and wings/fish bones and heads/shells from crustaceans
- 2 onions, quartered • 1 carrot, halved
- 1 stick of celery, halved
- 1 bouquet garni (1 bay leaf, 10 peppercorns, 5 parsley stalks, 2 sprigs of thyme)
- 1.5 litres *cold* water

Place the bones in a large heavy-based stockpot, cover with cold water and bring to a boil, uncovered. Remove the bones and rinse under cold running water to remove some of the impurities.

Place the bones in a clean stockpot with the rest of the ingredients and the measured water (use a little more if needed to cover the bones). Slowly bring to a simmer, uncovered. Using a large flat ladle, remove any scum which rises to the top. Simmer for 6 hours if making veal or beef stock, 4 hours for poultry. For fish, simmer for 45 minutes to 1 hour maximum.* Keep the pan uncovered and the bones submerged in liquid at all times, skimming occasionally and topping up with warm water if necessary.

Pour through a coffee filter or a fine sieve and chill.

* Pourquoi? It's important not to overcook fish stock as the brittle fish bones will start to dissolve calcium salts, which will cloud the stock and give it a chalky taste.

BROWN (ROASTED) STOCK
MAKES ABOUT I LITRE

- 1.5kg raw veal or beef knuckles or poultry carcasses, backs and wings*
- 2 tablespoons vegetable oil (a non-tasting oil, not olive oil)
- 2 onions, quartered with skin left on**
- 1 carrot, halved • 1 stick of celery, halved
- 1 bouquet garni (1 bay leaf, 10 peppercorns, 5 parsley stalks, 2 sprigs of thyme)
- 1.5 litres *cold* water

Preheat the oven to 200°C. Rub the bones with the oil and place them in a roasting tray with the vegetables. Roast for about an hour or until well browned.

Transfer the roasted bones and vegetables to a large heavy-based stockpot. Add the aromatics and the water (use a little more if needed to cover the bones) and slowly bring to a simmer, uncovered. Using a large flat ladle, remove any scum that rises to the top. Simmer for 6 hours for veal or beef stock, 4 hours for poultry, or until the stock has a strong flavour. Keep the pan uncovered and the bones submerged in liquid at all times, skimming occasionally and topping up with warm water if necessary.

Pour through a coffee filter or a fine sieve and chill.

* You can also use the carcasses from roast poultry and then roast the vegetables on their own at the beginning of the recipe.

** The onion skin enriches the colour of the stock.

Demi-glace

The old-fashioned version of *demi-glace* – equal parts roasted brown stock and espagnole sauce – is still seen on menus at fine dining restaurants. You can create a modern version by simply reducing brown (roasted) stock until thick enough to coat the back of a spoon. The gelatine will thicken the sauce, so there is no need for a thickening *roux*.

VEGETABLE STOCK
MAKES ABOUT I LITRE

- 1 tablespoon olive oil
- 2 onions, quartered with skin left on
- 3 cloves of garlic, pounded flat
- 2 carrots, roughly chopped
- 2 sticks of celery, roughly chopped
- ½ bulb of fennel, roughly chopped
- 2 tomatoes, roughly chopped
- 8 button mushrooms, brushed or peeled and roughly chopped
- 1 bouquet garni (1 bay leaf, 10 peppercorns, 5 parsley stalks, 2 sprigs of thyme)
- ½ teaspoon sugar • 1 teaspoon salt
- 1.5 litres *cold* water

Put all the ingredients, apart from the water, into a large heavy-based stockpot. Fry on a high heat for 10 minutes to soften and slightly brown the vegetables. Pour in the water (add more if needed to cover the vegetables) and slowly bring to a simmer. Simmer uncovered for 30 minutes. Let cool before straining through a coffee filter or a very fine sieve.

Sauces

L'ARBRE GÉNÉALOGIQUE FRANÇAIS DES SAUCES

THE FRENCH FAMILY TREE OF SAUCES

Sauces made the French kitchen famous and their history goes back to medieval times, but it was chef Antonin Carême (1784–1833) who classified them into four categories in *L'Art de la cuisine au XIXe siècle*. These 'mother sauces' are *béchamel* (creamy milk), *velouté* (white meat, fish or vegetables), *espagnole* (brown meat) and *tomate* (tomato), each of which can be turned into another 'secondary sauce' with a few extra ingredients. *Hollandaise* was created later, as the fifth and final mother sauce, and its spin-offs cover almost all forms of classic emulsions such as *mayonnaise* and *béarnaise*.

It doesn't matter whether you roast, grill, poach, barbecue or even serve some ingredients raw, a well-made sauce will take any meat, poultry, fish or vegetables to the next level. A sauce shouldn't mask a dish but enhance and bring out its flavours and, to avoid waste, sauces are a great way to make a delicious 'new' meal out of leftovers.

ROUX

A *roux* is a paste used for thickening sauces that consists of equal amounts of flour and butter (or sometimes pork or duck fat). It is cooked until it no longer tastes of flour or has achieved a certain colour, before the liquid for the sauce is added.

There are three different types of *roux*:

White: cooked without colouring until the flour is no longer raw. Used for *béchamel*-based sauces.

Blonde: cooked until a light golden colour. Used for *velouté*-based sauces.

Brown: cooked until almost a Coca-Cola colour and with a nutty taste. Used for *espagnole*-based sauces.

SAUCE BÉCHAMEL

SERVES 4–6 PEOPLE

A milk sauce thickened with a white *roux* and seasoned with onion, clove and bay. The easiest of the mother sauces, *béchamel* is a favourite for smothering almost anything and making it comforting – see the recipes for *Gratin au poisson fumé* (page 50) and *Endives au jambon* (page 159).

- 30g butter • 30g plain flour
- 500ml milk, lukewarm
- ¼ onion, skin removed • 1 clove • 1 bay leaf
- a pinch of nutmeg • salt and white pepper

Over a medium heat, melt the butter in a large pan and add the flour. Using a wooden spoon, beat hard to a smooth paste (*roux*). Take off the heat.

Start adding the milk to the *roux* by beating in about 2 tablespoons, then repeat until you have incorporated about a quarter of the milk. Switch to a whisk and gradually incorporate the rest of the milk.

Place the pan back over a medium heat and simmer with the onion, clove and bay leaf for 10 minutes. Whisk frequently to ensure that none of the sauce burns on the bottom of the pan. If the sauce becomes too thick (it should have the consistency of custard or a thick tomato sauce), whisk in a little more milk.

Remove the onion, clove and bay leaf, then add the nutmeg and season with salt and white pepper (black pepper is fine if you don't mind the speckles).

Mornay (cheese) sauce: before seasoning at the end, add 200g grated Gruyère or mature Comté cheese (or a strong hard cheese like Cheddar or Parmesan).

Creamy mustard sauce: stir in a generous tablespoon of grainy mustard before seasoning at the end.

Caper and parsley sauce: add 2 tablespoons chopped capers and a handful of chopped parsley before seasoning at the end.

VELOUTÉ SAUCES

These are made with a blonde *roux* as for a *béchamel* except that the milk is replaced by white unroasted stock or vegetable stock.

Velouté sauces are not served on their own but used as a base for a wide range of other sauces. Different stocks will influence the end result (vegetable stock making the lightest of sauces), and you can add chopped button mushrooms, fresh herbs such as tarragon and dill, or spices like paprika. Use your tastebuds and get creative!

Sauce Bercy below is a classic *velouté* sauce. For examples of other *velouté* sauces in action, see *Poulet aux champignons avec une sauce au vin blanc* (page 187) and *Asperges à la parisienne* (page 156).

SAUCE BERCY
SERVES 4 PEOPLE

Traditionally made with a fish *velouté* (blond *roux* plus fish stock) with shallots, butter and white wine but no cream. A perfect match for seafood.

- 2 shallots, finely chopped
- 2 knobs of butter • 125ml dry white wine
- salt • a few drops of lemon juice
- a handful of chopped parsley
- *For the velouté sauce* • 30g butter
- 30g plain flour • 450ml fish stock

To make the *velouté* sauce, melt the butter in a large pot over a medium heat and add the flour. Using a wooden spoon, beat hard until you have a smooth paste (*roux*). Continue to beat until the *roux* begins to have a light golden colour. Take off the heat.

Start adding the stock to the *roux* by beating in about 2 tablespoons, then repeat until you have incorporated about a quarter of the stock. Switch to a whisk and gradually incorporate the rest of the stock.

Place the pot back over a medium heat and simmer for 15–20 minutes. Whisk frequently to ensure that none of the sauce burns on the bottom of the pan. If the sauce becomes too thick (it should have the consistency of custard or a thick tomato sauce), whisk in a little more stock. Remove from the heat.

To finish, cook the shallots with a knob of butter in a large frying pan until translucent. Add the wine and reduce for 2 minutes before pouring in the *velouté* sauce. Simmer for 5 minutes. Season to taste with salt and lemon juice. Before serving, swirl in the remaining butter and add the chopped parsley.

SAUCE ESPAGNOLE
SERVES 4 PEOPLE

A classic in French cuisine, and the last time I counted I found over twenty different offspring. No wonder, when it's so versatile.

The classic *sauce espagnole* is reduced for several hours. This is my modern shortcut version, which can be served as it comes with roasted, grilled or poached meat, or you can add extra ingredients* to make a fine accompaniment to almost any dish.

- 30g *lardons* or cubes of smoked bacon**
- 1 onion, finely chopped
- 1 carrot, finely chopped
- 1 stick of celery, finely chopped
- 30g butter • 30g plain flour
- 500ml veal or beef stock, lukewarm
- 1 tablespoon tomato paste
- 1 bouquet garni (1 bay leaf, 10 peppercorns, 5 parsley stalks, 2 sprigs of thyme)

Over a medium heat, fry the *lardons* and vegetables until golden. Remove with a slotted spoon, trying to keep as much of the fat as possible in the pan. Melt the butter in the pan, sprinkle in the flour and stir constantly until it turns almost a Coca-Cola colour (this is a brown *roux*). Turn the heat down to low and slowly pour in the warm stock while whisking energetically. Once the stock is incorporated, add the tomato paste and whisk until dissolved. Pop the fried vegetables and *lardons* back into the pan, add the bouquet garni and simmer gently for 15 minutes. Pour through a sieve (to remove the vegetables, *lardons*, bouquet garni and any other bits) to make a silky-smooth sauce. Taste for seasoning.***

* *See the recipes for* Oeufs en meurette *(page 26), and* Saucisse et purée de pomme de terre avec une sauce diable *(page 69).*

** *If you prefer not to use pork, replace the lardons with 1 tablespoon butter.*

*** *If you like, stir in 2–3 tablespoons crème fraîche just before tasting for seasoning.*

TOMATO SAUCES

These no-fuss sauces are good back-up recipes. They can be prepared in advance and even frozen.

ESCOFFIER'S TOMATO SAUCE
SERVES 4–6 PEOPLE

You may think that the Italians have mastered the art of tomato sauces but Escoffier's* is a pretty mean sauce too. The addition of *lardons* and veal stock gives it a deep, meaty-rich flavour, and you can add a dash of double cream or knob of butter before serving if you wish.

This is my adaptation of Escoffier's classic recipe.

- 30g butter
- 1 clove of garlic, crushed to a paste
- 50g *lardons* or cubes of smoked bacon
- 1 carrot, chopped into medium dice
- 1 onion, finely chopped • 30g plain flour
- 500ml veal or beef stock, lukewarm
- 1kg tomatoes, roughly chopped
- a pinch of sugar, or to taste • salt and pepper

Melt the butter in a large pan. Add the garlic, *lardons*, carrot and onion and sweat on a medium heat for 10 minutes or until the vegetables are soft and some of the fat from the *lardons* has melted. Sprinkle in the flour and cook for a further couple of minutes, then whisk continuously while slowly pouring in the stock.

Add the tomatoes and simmer, covered, for an hour or until they have broken down completely.

Whizz the sauce in an electric blender until smooth. Season to taste with the sugar, salt and pepper.

* Auguste Escoffier (1846–1935) modernized and popularized French cooking as we know it today. In 1903 he published Le Guide culinaire, *which is still regarded as a major reference work for professional cooks, both for recipes and kitchen management. Drawing on his experience in the French army, Escoffier organized the kitchen team by hierarchy of authority, responsibility and function, with each individual delegated a specific task. This system is still used throughout the restaurant world today.*

MODERN TOMATO SAUCE (VEGAN)
SERVES 2–3 PEOPLE

- 1 onion, finely chopped
- 1 carrot, finely chopped
- 1 stick of celery, finely chopped
- 1 clove of garlic, crushed to a paste
- 2 tablespoons olive oil
- 500g tinned tomatoes, chopped
- a pinch of sugar • salt and pepper

Sweat the onion, carrot, celery and garlic with the olive oil for 10 minutes or until tender. Add the chopped tomatoes and simmer, covered, for an hour.

Whizz the sauce in an electric blender until smooth. Season to taste with the sugar, salt and pepper.

SAUCES AU BEURRE
BUTTER SAUCES

These simple sauces are probably the quickest way to add extra flavour to fish (see *Poisson meunière* on page 180), meat, poultry and vegetables. There's not much to them, apart from melting a little butter.

BEURRE BLANC
SERVES 2–3 PEOPLE

- 1 shallot, finely chopped
- 6 tablespoons dry white wine
- 4 tablespoons white wine vinegar
- 4 tablespoons double cream
- 100g butter, cubed
- salt • a pinch of cayenne pepper

Simmer the shallot, wine and vinegar in a pan until reduced to 1 tablespoon. Remove the pan from the heat and whisk in the cream followed by a cube of butter at a time. Make sure to whisk energetically. If the butter isn't melting, put the pan back on a low heat. Once all the butter is incorporated, season with salt and a little cayenne. Serve immediately.

Chopped herbs, such as mint, parsley, basil or tarragon, make a nice addition.

BEURRE NOISETTE
SERVES 2 PEOPLE

- 100g butter, cubed
- 1 tablespoon chopped parsley

Put the butter into a large pan and place on a medium heat. Cook until the butter has become a nutty brown colour, then remove from the heat and add the parsley. Serve immediately.

BEURRE AU CITRON
SERVES 2 PEOPLE

- juice of 1 lemon • 4 tablespoons dry white wine
- 100g butter, cubed • salt

Simmer the lemon juice and wine in a pan until reduced to 1 tablespoon. Remove the pan from the heat and whisk in the butter a cube at a time. Make sure to whisk energetically. If the butter isn't melting, put the pan back on a low heat. Once all the butter is incorporated, season with a little salt. Serve immediately.

LES ÉMULSIONS
DRESSINGS

These use liquids that don't normally bind together easily. They are combined by rapid mixing to make them smooth, and are renowned for being the trickiest of sauces to make. With my recipes and a few tips and tricks, though, they should be a doddle.

HOLLANDAISE
SERVES 2–3 PEOPLE

Although the name suggests Dutch origins, historians claim that *sauce hollandaise* was a French invention most likely dating from the mid-eighteenth century. Hollandaise sauce and asparagus is like mint and peas – a match made in heaven – but hollandaise can be served with other vegetables too (it's particularly nice with long-stemmed purple broccoli that can be dipped into the sauce).

- 3 egg yolks, at room temperature
- 200g butter, melted and still warm
- juice of ½ lemon • salt and pepper

Place a large heatproof bowl over a pot of simmering water. Put the egg yolks into the bowl and whisk them at the same time as adding the melted warm butter, drop by drop. Whisk constantly* until the sauce has the consistency of thick cream. Take off the heat, add the lemon juice and season to taste. Use immediately.

* *Make sure to whisk constantly and vigorously as this helps to disperse the water and oil droplets evenly, and so stop the sauce separating.*

Sauce Béarnaise: Place 6 tablespoons each dry white wine and white wine vinegar in a pan with 10 peppercorns and a finely chopped shallot. Simmer until reduced by half. Strain and leave to cool for a couple of minutes (it should be lukewarm, not boiling), then whisk into the finished hollandaise sauce followed by 2 tablespoons chopped tarragon. (If you replace the tarragon with mint, you will have a sauce paloise, which is great with lamb and mutton.)

Sauce Maltaise: Simmer 100ml orange juice in a pan until reduced to about 2 tablespoons. Fold into the finished hollandaise sauce with the finely grated zest of 1 unwaxed orange. Check for seasoning.

Sauce Mousseline: Whisk 1 egg white to soft peaks and fold into the finished hollandaise sauce. Check for seasoning.

MAYONNAISE
SERVES 2–3 PEOPLE

- 3 egg yolks, at room temperature
- 200–250ml sunflower or vegetable oil*
- a few drops of white wine vinegar or lemon juice • salt

Place the egg yolks in a large glass or stainless steel bowl set on a damp tea towel (this will stop the bowl from slipping). Start by whisking the egg yolks a little, then add the oil drop by drop until the eggs begin to thicken and become pale in colour.

Continue by drizzling the oil into the mix until you have achieved the consistency you like. Add a few drops of white wine vinegar or lemon juice and season with salt.

If you would like your mayonnaise to have the peppery taste of olive oil, switch to an extra virgin olive oil when the mixture has become thick and pale in colour. I find using only olive oil gives the mayonnaise a bitter taste.

Chopped fresh herbs, such as parsley, dill, tarragon or basil, make a great addition to mayonnaise.

If you like a little heat, why not try adding a little wasabi, harissa or sweet chilli sauce?

Sauce Tartare: Mix 1 tablespoon each chopped capers, cornichons, parsley, tarragon and chervil into the mayonnaise.

Sauce Cocktail: Mix 1 tablespoon tomato ketchup into the mayonnaise with 1 teaspoon each Cognac and Worcestershire sauce and a dash of Tabasco or a pinch of cayenne pepper.

VINAIGRETTE

MAKES ENOUGH FOR A
GREEN SALAD TO SERVE 4–6

Vinaigrette wasn't always associated with salad dressings. From the late eighteenth century until the middle of the nineteenth, it was the name given to a small box made of gold, mother-of-pearl or ivory. Fashionable ladies of the time wore the box on a necklace and inside they kept a small sponge soaked in aromatic vinegar. The sponge was used to dab foreheads and temples when the ladies felt flushed.

I think a much better way of handling hot flushes is to eat a perfectly dressed fresh green salad. The French know how to dress, both in fashion and salad terms. They keep it simple and classic.

A ratio of 3 parts oil to 1 part acid is a general rule of thumb when making *vinaigrette*, but at the end of the day your personal taste can always make it a little more or less acidic.

Once you know the basics, feel free to add different types of mustard to your *vinaigrette*, or chopped herbs, shallots or chilli. For other ideas, see the recipe for *Salade de carottes râpées et rémoulade de céleri-rave et pommes* (page 110).

- 6 tablespoons oil*
- 2 tablespoons vinegar or lemon juice
- 1 teaspoon salt
- a generous pinch of sugar

Use an empty clean jar to shake the oil and vinegar, or whisk them together in a bowl, making sure they blend together well. Season with the salt and sugar. Try the dressing by dipping in a salad leaf and tasting, then adjust the seasoning to your liking if necessary. As long as it doesn't contain herbs, *vinaigrette* will keep in an airtight container in a cool cupboard for months, although it will need to be stirred or shaken (if kept in a jar) before using.

Vegetable or sunflower oil will give the dressing a delicate taste, whereas extra virgin olive oil is more robust in flavour. I find a combination of both works well. You can also experiment with other oils that have a distinctive taste, such as hazelnut, pistachio and pumpkin.

How to make your own vinegar

If you're like me and sometimes end up with leftover wine and don't know what to do with it, you could have a go at making your own vinegar (although you can freeze wine in an ice-cube tray and use it for cooking later). Home-made vinegar is easy, and tends to have a more complex flavour than the bought varieties.

You will need equal amounts of red wine* and organic cider vinegar (or live vinegar).** Stir them together and pour into a clean large container with a loose-fitting lid, making sure there's enough room for air to circulate. Cover with a piece of cheesecloth and then the lid and store in a cool, dark place for 1 week.

Remove the lid and cheesecloth and take a sniff – it should have a dominate smell and taste of vinegar with a light aroma of wine. It can be used at this stage, but it will develop more flavour if left for another week. When you need vinegar for kitchen use, pour some off and then top up the base with new wine. The vinegar will continue to develop more flavour the longer you leave it and can be kept in a dark cupboard for six months.

White wine or Champagne can be used instead of red wine.

** *Pourquoi? Organic cider vinegar contains live bacteria that turn the wine into vinegar.*

Crème pâtissière

PASTRY CREAM
MAKES ABOUT 600G

PREPARATION TIME: 20 MINUTES
RESTING TIME: I HOUR
COOKING TIME: 20 MINUTES

Crème pâtissière ('pastry cream') might not sound like the most exciting French dessert recipe but it is a great one to know.

Once you have the hang of making it, there'll be no stopping you. Fill éclairs, millefeuilles, tarts, cakes, doughnuts, trifles or fold in some whipped cream to make a a simple mousse or, as the French call it, a *crème Madame*. The possibilities are endless. And then there are also countless flavours: vanilla, chocolate, coffee, orange, cinnamon. You could probably incorporate pastry cream into any dessert, it's that versatile. It can also be made in advance and kept in the fridge for 2–3 days. *Café Gourmande* (pages 212–15) is a great example of the versatility of *crème pâtissière*. All you have to do is make one quantity of the basic recipe and with a couple of extra ingredients you can then create three mini desserts: strawberry and vanilla tartelettes, orange mousse and *crème de cassis* trifle. Ssssssshhhhh, don't tell anyone how simple it is, though – your friends will be less impressed.

- 120g egg yolks (roughly 6 medium egg yolks)
- 100g caster sugar
- 40g cornstarch • 1 vanilla pod*
- 500ml whole milk

Whisk the egg yolks with the sugar until light and thick, then whisk in the cornstarch.

Split the vanilla pod in half and scrape out the grains, using the back of a knife. Add the vanilla pod and grains (or your choice of flavouring) to the milk. Bring the milk to a boil and switch off the heat. Remove the vanilla pod and pour the milk in a slow stream on to the egg mixture, whisking vigorously all the time.

Return the mixture to a clean pot and continuously whisk over a medium heat. Make sure to scrape the sides and the bottom, otherwise it will burn. The cream will start to thicken. Once it releases a bubble or two, take it off the heat.

Pour on to a tray lined with cling film. Cover with cling film (pat the cling film so it sticks directly on to the cream) and refrigerate for at least an hour before using.

* Instead of a vanilla pod, try these other flavours:

Chocolate: *2 heaped tablespoons cocoa powder*

Coffee: *2 teaspoons instant coffee powder*

Mocha: *2 teaspoons instant coffee powder, I heaped tablespoon cocoa powder*

Citrus: *zest of I orange, lemon, lime or a combination of all three*

Lavender: *I teaspoon of dried lavender (remove from the infused milk before incorporating with the eggs)*

Tea: *2 heaped tablespoons Earl Grey, green or matcha tea (remove from the infused milk before incorporating with the eggs)*

Spices: *try cinnamon, ginger, tonka bean, nutmeg, chilli (works particularly well with chocolate)*

Cook's Notes

Unless otherwise stated, I've used the following ingredients in the recipes:

- *coarse sea salt*
- *freshly ground black pepper*
- *freshly grated nutmeg*
- *full-fat milk*
- *unsalted butter*
- *caster sugar*
- *medium-sized eggs, fruit and vegetables*
- *bouquet garni: 1 bay leaf, 10 peppercorns, 5 parsley stalks, 2 sprigs of thyme*

Spoon measures are level unless otherwise stated

- *1 teaspoon = 5ml*
- *1 tablespoon = 15ml*

Centigrade temperatures are given for conventional ovens. For fan-assisted ovens reduce the temperature by 20°C. For other ovens, see the conversion chart on the opposite page.

Weights

7.5 g	¼ oz	85 g	3 oz	340 g	12 oz	1.1 kg	2½ lb
15 g	½ oz	100 g	3½ oz	370 g	13 oz	1.4 kg	3 lb
20 g	¾ oz	115 g	4 oz	400 g	14 oz	1.5 kg	3½ lb
30 g	1 oz	140 g	5 oz	425 g	15 oz	1.8 kg	4 lb
35 g	1¼ oz	170 g	6 oz	455 g	1 lb	2 kg	4½ lb
40 g	1½ oz	200 g	7 oz	565 g	1¼ lb	2.3 kg	5 lb
50 g	1¾ oz	225 g	8 oz	680 g	1½ lb	2.7 kg	6 lb
55 g	2 oz	255 g	9 oz	795 g	1¾ lb	3.1 kg	7 lb
65 g	2¼ oz	285 g	10 oz	905 g	2 lb	3.6 kg	8 lb
70 g	2½ oz	310 g	11 oz	1 kg	2 lb 3 oz	4.5 kg	10 lb

Oven Temperatures

Very cool	110°C	225°F	Gas ¼
Very cool	130°C	250°F	Gas ½
Cool	140°C	275°F	Gas 1
Slow	150°C	300°F	Gas 2
Moderately slow	160°C	325°F	Gas 3
Moderate	180°C	350°F	Gas 4
Moderately hot	190°C	375°F	Gas 5
Hot	200°C	400°F	Gas 6
Very hot	220°C	425°F	Gas 7
Very hot	230°C	450°F	Gas 8
Hottest	240°C	475°F	Gas 9

Mon carnet d'adresses parisiennes

My Paris addresses

It's impossible to list all the amazing foodie places in Paris, so I've just popped my regulars down.

Le Bal café

It's not often you find two women running a restaurant in Paris and even more unusual to find two Englishwomen. They cook up a storm with their English dishes with a French twist. It's not just the Brit expats like me who are loving their cooking; the French are too.

6 Impasse de la Défense
75018 Paris

Le Baratin

Off a little sidestreet in Paris's second Chinatown, Belleville, you'll find this restaurant serving simple, tasty French food and a great selection of wines.

3 rue Jouye Rouve
75020 Paris

Le Baron rouge

After all that hard work doing the food shopping, I like to pop into this charming wine bar which is just off marché d'Aligre. At the weekend they serve oysters in addition to a great plate of charcuterie or cheese.

1 rue Théophile Roussel
75012 Paris

Bob's juice bar

www.bobsjuicebar.com

When I need a break from French food, I like to pop by Bob's for a juice and a healthy salad.

15 rue Lucien Sampaix
75010 Paris

Boucherie Leclerc

My local butchers, who are always serving with a smile and happy to give me some advice on how to cook the meat perfectly.

53 rue Meaux
75019 Paris

Café Chéri(e)

My local. Not typically Parisian, being right in the heart of the second Chinatown in Paris, but it makes for interesting people-watching.

44 Boulevard de la Villette
75019 Paris

Le Chateaubriand

Diners put their appetites into chef Inaki Aizpitarte's very capable hands with his evening fixed menu. A little difficult to get a reservation but you can turn up before 9 p.m. and wait at the bar for a table to become available.

129 avenue Parmentier
75011 Paris

La Cocotte

www.lacocotte.net

Cute culinary store selling their own cooking accessories (tea towels) and a small selection of well-chosen cookbooks.

5 rue Paul Bert
75011 Paris

G. Detou

If you're looking for 5kg bags of blanched almonds or a 10kg bag of chocolate buttons, then this is a place for you. Stocked with a huge range of French delicacies (not all in large bags). I guarantee it'll be hard to walk out the door empty handed.

58 rue Tiquetonne
75002 Paris

Du pain et des idées

www.dupainetdesidees.com

They do great little rolls with different fillings (*lardons*, cheese, sundried tomatoes, figs . . .) and their pain des amis is very good too.

34 rue Yves Toudic
75010 Paris

L'échoppée locale

www.echoppee-locale.fr

This little grocery store specializes in products just from the Ile-de-France region. I especially like their pear cider.

237 rue Saint Martin
75003 Paris

Gontran Cherrier

www.gontrancherrierboulanger.com

The charming French baker from pages 112–15.

22 rue Caulaincourt
75018 Paris

Le Grain du riz

If you're fed up with the typical French service, this tiny Vietnamese restaurant (virtually the size of a rice grain) serves genuine delicious Vietnamese food with a warm, friendly smile.

49 rue Godefroy Cavaignac
75011 Paris

Ma cave en ville

My local wine dealer. A great selection of wine with a lot of hard-to-find, organic and natural wines.

105 rue Belleville
75019 Paris

Marché d'Aligre

Each neighbourhood will have a fresh produce market once or twice a week (apart from Mondays). The marché d'Aligre is open Tuesday–Sunday mornings. The selection is large, with covered and open-air areas, plus there are some great North African grocery stores.

Rue d'aligre
75012 Paris

Mora

www.mora.fr

This store is a treasure trove for any budding chef. A little pricey, but all the products sold in the store are of good quality. In the same street there are a few other chef stores: A. Simon and Bovida.

13 rue Montmartre
75001 Paris

À la petite fabrique du chocolat

This little chocolate shop was just around the corner from my first apartment in Paris, which wasn't a very good thing. My favourite is their dark chocolate praline bar. *C'est tellement terrible* (it's so bad, delicious) that I even managed to eat a whole bar in one sitting.

12 rue Saint-Sabin
75011 Paris

Septime

Young chef Bertrand Grébaut won a grant from Evian-Badoit to open up his restaurant and realize his dream of making *haute cuisine* accessible to everyone. I love his modern take on French food using the best seasonal ingredients.

80 rue Charonne
75011 Paris

Index

Remerciements

Acknowledgements

This book would have never happened if my editor, Lindsey Evans, hadn't responded to my 'cold-call' email and given thirty minutes of her time for me to pitch my 'Little Paris Kitchen' cookbook idea (a special thank you to Sarah Canet at Spoon PR for giving me her email address). Lindsey, thanks for taking a chance on me and supporting me in writing my French classics.

Thanks also to:

John Hamilton: your enthusiasm and vision have made this book something special.

David Loftus: for being as excited as me about doing this book and of course for making the food (and me) look stunning.

The Penguin team: *merci à tous* for your devotion and eagerness to make this book a success.

Elodie Rambaud: your 'cute' touches have made this book beautiful.

Frankie Unsworth: you're the best culinary assistant in the world and the best foodie partner in crime, too!

Lizzy Kremer and the team at David Higham: thanks for always being on call.

Un grand merci to all of my guests who came for lunch at La petite cuisine à Paris. And to all of those who tried to come, I wish I could have had you all over for lunch.

Lana and Misha Citron: without you guys, I would have never made it on to the Eurostar with all my luggage when I moved to Paris. Lana, your encouragement and faith in me has helped me enormously over the years.

Benjamin Rurka: thanks for always believing that I'll make it.

Kami, Loïs, Claire et Bertrand Soleil: *merci mille fois* for making me feel at home and showing me the Parisian way of life when I first moved here.

Andrea Wainer: *merci* for giving me my first culinary job in Paris and opening up a whole world of new opportunities.

My friends (or rather, my recipe guinea pigs!): thanks for being up for eating my experiments (even if they weren't always that delicious).

Many thanks to Astier de Villatte (www.astierdevillatte.com) and to Le Creuset (www.lecreuset.fr) for the lovely props.

And finally, my family, who have been there through thick and thin. Without your love and support, I wouldn't be where I am now.

LES FEUILLES DE LAURIER

LE THON

LES AMANDES

LE CAHIER

LA VAISSELLE

LE FENOU

LE FOUR

L'HUITRE

LES CHANTERELLES

LA COCOTTE

LA CARAFE D'EAU

LE POULE

LE PASTIS

LES FROMAGES

LE COCKTAIL

LE TIRE BOUCHON

LES POMMES DE TERRE

LE CÈPE

LE BOL

LES POIVRONS

LE GÂTEAU

LA RHUBARBE

LA SALADE

L'ORAN

LE SUCRE

LA LAVANDE

LE SANDWICH

LE MOULIN À POIVRE

LES PIMENTS

LA FARIN

LA POIRE

LES ALLUMETTES

LE PANIER

LE ROMARIN

LE THÉ

LA MENTH

LE LAIT

UNE PLANCHE À DÉCOUPER

LE ROULEAU À PÂTISSERIE

LES ABEILLES

LE SAC À DOS

LA BAGUETTE

LES SERVIETTES

LES OIGNONS FRAIS

L'HUILE D'OLIVE

L'ARBRE

LE CITRON

LE SAUCISSON